AF424065

Richard Kyere-Boateng

To order additional copies of
Believing Yourself, the Beginning of Greatness
Call +233-242-876622 / +233-505-755110

Write to
Richard Kyere-Boateng
P. O. Box ABK 197, Abuakwa Kumasi, Ghana
kyerebee@gmail.com
http://richiepeepublications.com

Printed April 2019
ISBN 978-9988-2-9634-6
Published by Richie Pee Publications

Typesetters
Agyeiwaa Kyere-Boateng
Leticia Asante Appiah
Richard Kyere-Boateng

Editor
Richard Kyere-Boateng

Cover Designer
Richard Kyere-Boateng

Photographers
Richard Kyere-Boateng
Agyeiwaa Kyere-Boateng

It will inspire, nurture and motivate you to believe yourself, by taking the initiative and beginning to have a change of mindset. When you start believing yourself, you will see greatness in your life at a study pace.

Richard Kyere-Boateng
BA. Communication Design
Diploma in Education

Contents

Dedication

This book is dedicated to my children Agyeiwaa, Tiwaa, Queenstar, Boatemaa and my wife Leticia Asante Appiah, for their love, prayers and unflinching support that gave me the zeal to finish the book.

Foreword

In recent years, man has been battling with ways of managing negativity, believing yourself, will give you the necessary power to strive for excellence.

This book has come at the right moment, because it will provide you with the needed motivations that will urge you to crave for excellence. Today, most of the youth are not making much impact in life, because of negative mindset, taken over their minds.

That is why, I wish to entreat you to acquaint yourself with the book, *"Believing Yourself the Beginning of Greatness"* to help in your personal development and career life.

After reading it, your life will never be the same, because it will graduate you from self-doubt to self-believe where the greatness in you will begin.

Pr. Theophilus Appiah Mensah
Publishing Director North Ghana Mission
of Seventh-day Adventist Church

Preface

Life from the standpoint of a negative-minded person is perceived as frustrating, stressful and miserable. Therefore, you must do all you can to avoid negativity or at least manage the influx of negative words in your life, if you really want to reach great heights.

During my days as a teenager, negativity engulfed me like a flame of fire. It nearly killed my dreams and aspirations. Life was no more interesting, at a point in time, I wished the world would end for me to be free from the excruciating pain of negativity. I lost my self-confidence, I thought I had a dream of becoming a great motivational speaker, but the views of some insignificant persons trapped my effort and I ended up in the servitude of negativity. The passion I had to pursue my dreams vanished into thin air, as a result, the dreams and aspirations I had in mind nearly came to an abrupt end.

Later in life, I had a wake-up call from people who saw my potentials and revealed it to me. Other sources like radio programs, inspirational books and videos took over my words, actions and emotions. The pendulum of life within my social circle swung from silly negative comments, to inspiring positive vibes, which finally turned my life around.

After several years of teaching at a senior high school, I have realized that, some students do not do well, in their academic pursuit, due to low self-esteem. This happened as a result, of negative mindset taking over their words, actions and emotions, as they battle with life in their quest of achieving academic excellence.

What I have noticed over the years is that, everything that you can do as an individual, stemmed from the mind. If you can train your mind to develop positive mindset, it may lead to the beginning of greatness, in your life. This inspired me to write this book *"Believing Yourself the Beginning of Greatness"* to help inspire students in high schools, colleges and the working class, who have the burning desires to aspire to the top, to use it as a source of inspiration to keep their dreams alive. It will also help them to know their purpose in life, the need to have a positive mindset and urge them to believe themselves, as they clear all negative thoughts in their journey to greatness.

Finally, the book will assist students in their search for the right career path, through personal development, while aiding them to uncover their skills, abilities and interests, which will direct, inspire and nurture them, in their quest of achieving greatness.

Richard Kyere-Boateng
Teacher, Ghana Education Service
Bawku Senior High School

"You Can Change Your Status quo, by Just Believing Yourself and Soon, Your Effort Will Turn Your Believes into Achievable Goals."
Richard Kyere-Boateng
Believing YOURSELF, the Beginning of GREATNESS

CHAPTER ONE

The Need to Believe Yourself

Great ideas mostly come to each individual as mental pictures, believing yourself can stimulate you to turn these pictures into reality, where people can see and feel its benefits.

However, many people do not believe themselves and rather allow negative comments, emanating from negative minds, to undermine the little effort they are making. At times, some individuals often don't know that, when you believe in yourself as a person, it can lead you to greatness. It seems that they are oblivious to the fact that, once individuals believe themselves, no external obstacles can stop them from achieving their dreams and aspirations.

For the most part of our lives, we normally seek external motivations, whereas internal motivations elude us. This may be attributed to negligence on the part of us, since we normally underestimate self-doubt, not knowing that self-doubt can lead to low self-esteem and further cause individuals to live below their optimum. That is why believing yourself can inspire you as an individual to live beyond your wildest dreams. The fact is that, deep within you as an individual, you may know yourself better than anyone else may know. Since you are the driver of your own life, you can change your status quo, by just believing yourself and soon, your effort will turn your believes into

achievable goals. Therefore, if you finally discover yourself, your internal motivations will then lead you to greatness.

Your believing power, will give you the extra urge to overcome adversity. Henceforth, it would be highly impossible for someone to discourage you from pursuing your dream. Believing will instil in you a formidable spirit that will urge you to press on, even when obstacle seems unsurmountable. It will equip you to fight vigorously, against any problem that may crop up, by focusing on one's mindset, capability and passion.

However, believing yourself, will gradually lead you to believe in things you possess like your skills, talents and abilities, which may finally give you the can do spirit, to forge ahead. Believing yourself is the starting point to all greatness because it will urge you to create, innovate and solve nagging problems surfacing within your environs.

As you begin each day, in your quest of achieving your purpose in life, identifying your abilities can help you set realistic goals that relate to your competencies. Since believing yourself, resonates with what you can do, achieving these goals, will be as easy as ABC, which will then enable you to live your life to the fullness.

If you have never thought of believing yourself, I will entreat you to try without hesitation, for if you do, it will be a complete makeover of your life, since it will propel you towards your goals and aspirations. When the opportunity opens, your believing power will inspire you to live a determine lifestyle that will lead you to greatness.

The Benefits of believing yourself are listed below, nonetheless, you can derive it, only when you begin to believe yourself that most dreams you envisage, can happen in your lifetime.

1. **Your confidence level will increase**

In life, things that trigger confidence begin with a believing mentality that, you are somebody and worth something. If your mindset begins to move in this direction, your confidence level will rise. You will then, care less about the utterances of insignificant persons, who always try to prevent you from achieving greatness.

When you begin to believe yourself, it will give you the power to build and nurture confidence within yourself. This can serve as a shield to protect you, while giving you the power to achieve something significant. As your confidence level go higher and higher, you will begin to believe yourself and aspiring to great heights will not be any strange thing to you.

Confidence will be something that resonates with you. Hence, it will then manifest itself in everything you do. As you believe yourself, you will speak, walk and talk confidently, as and when life demands it.

Confidence will give you the cutting edge to take leadership role and excel. It will urge you to connect with your audience and make a significant impact in their lives as you stand to address them. Through confidence, you will acquire the power to plan, organize and direct your subordinates. Having confidence means you believe yourself. This believe, will serve as a stimulant that will arouse your adrenaline to hit the ground running, with all the zeal you need in order to reach the destination set by you.

Bear in mind that, confidence is not a one-time achievement, but is a skill, that may develop gradually, through practice. As you continue to practise, you will soon get the hang of it, while your confidence level build-up overtime. This goes to buttress the assertion that practice makes perfect. As you strive hard to increase your confidence level, this will gradually move you towards greatness.

2. You will realize your potentials

As you begin to believe yourself, little by little you will progress steadily, in the quest of knowing your potentials. When you start believing yourself, things will begin to fall into place, while you acquire an open mind to uncover the potentials you possess. Eventually, friends and acquaintances will also see the potentials you have. If you believe yourself, it will urge you to utilize several opportunities that may come your way without hesitation. The role you will play, will lead you to discover most of the hidden abilities, skills and interest you never knew you have. When these potentials come to the full glare of others, a door of greatness will open for you.

When you begin to believe yourself, it will break all impediments on your way to success and make it easier, for you to experience greatness. You will begin to believe every choice or decision made by you. This will urge you to believe in your own initiatives that will lead you to greatness. It will interest you to know in life that at times, people will pass their comments, opinions or criticisms, but the onus rest on the way you see yourself or react to situations, the choices you make and how you arrive at decisions. These may often have an impact on your working life.

One antidote you should know is that, as you believe yourself, it will urge you to trust your instinct and build your self-confidence that will help you surpass any negative utterances that will surround you. The crux of the matter is that, as you continue to navigate through life each day, with the principles of believing yourself, most of the things you will do, will gradually bear fruit. As you continue with these principles, the potentials you have realize within you, will lead you to greatness. Others, who do not know your source of inspiration, will be having different views about your achievement. However, deep within you, the true source of your driving power, that drives you like no one else do, certainly will be your believing power.

3. **You will rub shoulders with the elite in society**

Once you believe yourself, you will value your persona as a great person. From that moment onwards, you will think and act as a great person. Believing yourself, will urge you to move and rub shoulders with great personalities of your generation. Their believing power will equipped you with the zeal you need, without showing any sign of negativity with regard to your personality. This may happen due to, the similar attributes you share with the elite in the community in which you found yourself.

Henceforth, there will not be much difference between great people and you, due to the confidence and self-believe instilled in you. As your self-believe

takes, you to several places, renowned and pundits will begin to notice you. When it happens like that, where praises is due, they will do so and where constructive criticism is needed too, they will not hesitate to air their views, when opportunity presents itself. This will give you the chance to meet and interact with these great personalities of your generation, when you tap into their experience.

It can only be possible with just believe at the beginning of anything you want to start. If you allow yourself belief to spearhead every move you make, you will soon reach your goals.

4. You will be a role model to others

Many people will look up to you and draw inspirations from you, because of the confidence you have shown in the discharge of your duties. This will give you the trust, hope and respect that every role model offers. When others begin to look up to you as a role model, their actions will boost your confidence level as they encourage and urge you to continue to make strive in life without looking back.

It will be a great asset to you, since believing yourself will lead you to new heights. Many will see you as a mentor and count on your experience. As a result, you will be an asset to your friends, community and the world as a whole, if you continue to press on with the believing power you have nurtured overtime.

5. You will excel in all your endeavours

Even in the midst of stubborn critics, their master plan of bringing you down will not hold water. Due to the innate skills, believes and the confidence you repose in yourself, it will be difficult to pander to the prejudice of your adversaries, because their master plan will fail right in front of you. This will open a door of success for you, since stiff oppresses will not succeed in their quest of bringing you down. When you continue to believe in yourself, the sky's the limit for you, since your believe will let everything you touch flourish. Through the self-believe, the tools for excelling to a greater height will be at your doorstep.

6. You will be a blessing to others

Your unflinching support for others, will pave the way for them to experience a better life and inspire them to take initiative, to enable them earn livelihood for themselves.

Consequently, most of them will forever be grateful, once you help them out. Your advice and motivation may change the lives of your friends, your community and the world as a whole. When your little believes resonate with them, most of them will begin an initiative on their own, through the positive influence you have on them.

Once you focus on the positive side of life, coupled with your ideas, plans and strategies, these will take you to places, where you least expect to be. The little believes that you have, can be of paramount importance to thousands of people, who will draw from your strength to realize their agenda on earth. So do not allow comments from negative minds limit your ideas and demean your personality.

It may interest you to know that, deep within these negative-minded persons, your positive attributes may not be open to them. Therefore, keep your flames of greatness burning, in order to be a blessing to others, when the need arises.

7. You can easily surmount obstacles

Surmounting obstacles will no longer be a herculean task since believing yourself, will offer you many ways through which these challenges can be solved. When you allow self-believe to take a centre stage of your mind, you will often tackle issues with a positive mindset that will aid you to figure out several ways of solving problems. This will offer you, a broader perspective in tackling issues, whereby series of answers will come to your mind, not just one solution.

Eventually, you will have an upper hand in solving issues easily than a colleague, who does not believe himself and tend to complain when troubles crop up. When you begin to solve problems daily with little or no effort, you will build network of friends and acquaintances, who will trust in you and your capabilities. They will then whisper your smartness and ingenuity to others.

As days go by, if you continue to portray the believing power in you and draw closer to achieving the unachievable each day, it may open a window of opportunity in your life.

Those who do not value the power of believing yourself will experience a shock as you move from just a modicum of success to greatness.

8. You will move from fixed mindset to growth mindset

Growth mindset stem from the fact that, no matter how worse your situation has reached now, it will improve overtime. If you believe yourself, you may grow from whatever project, subject or courses you are embarking on to new heights, by just believing yourself. This mindset will urge you to continue unabated with yourself-believe. When you continue to press on, you will achieve the results you have been waiting for. This alone will be enough to motivate you within yourself, as impediments meet you in your journey to greatness.

When you navigate through life with a growth mindset, you will experience greatness in anything you set your mind on, since you are likely to tackle issues with a learned-mind, which will help you capture ideas and knowledge from one stage to the other. Growth mindset will let you grow steadily until you reach your peak where the greatness in you will appear.

9. You will experience a paradigm shift in your finances

Believing yourself will give you a discipline mindset that will change the financial constraints you are experiencing now and take you to the world of financial liberty. When you experience financial liberty, it will give you the purchasing power that may serve as an added advantage to help you spread your

tentacles to other places where your dream may touch millions of people in diverse cultures.

At this point in time, it may be prudent to do all you can and stay away from negative minds, else these defeatists mentality, will retard your mental faculty. So when such time comes, stay within the confines of the believe systems that has worked for you so far.

Once you take these steps towards achieving your goals in life, no matter how long it takes, you will surely get there. It is better late than never to hit the ground running, until you achieve your desires. If you fail to do so, the devastating effect of your inactions is outline below, acquaint yourself with it and take a decision.

1. **You will be tag as a loser**

   Many people will see you as a loser, since you fail to salvage yourself from the shackles of life. They will then begin to question your competencies in other facets of life. At any point in time, those who live with you in the same vicinity will finally draw conclusion and call you a loser.

   The fact is that, you fail to take the initiative that could have change your present condition hence, your hard-earned name would gradually dwindled to its barest minimum.

2. **You will live within your means**

   Low self-esteem and lack of self-belief will plunge you into a state of financial chaos, where the pressures of life will force you, to live within your means. Since you are not taking any action to cause things to happen in your life, your progression toward success will be motionless. Things will rather cause you pain and agony, instead of you causing things to happen the way you desire.

3. You will not be recognized

When the day of reckoning comes, while dignitaries are revered and awarded according to their actions, your name will not be found on the list of people who deserved recognition. This will happen because of your inactions over the years. You will then be out of the limelight, which will make it difficult for others to notice your existence and the contributions you have made. As a result, your own family and community will not recognized you, because you are not making any serious impact in the lives of others.

Stand up and face the realities of life with a sense of purpose, to prove to the world that, you have what it takes to be different, in order to make significant changes within you, your community and the world as a whole.

4. Your lifetime legacy will be in shambles

The childhood legacy you have nurtured all this while and wish to leave behind as your legacy will be in shambles: due to your inactions, indecision and laziness. If you do not recognized, these mistakes, by making conscious effort to change your status quo, all your dreams will go down the drain.

Remember the ball is in your court now, rise up and change your status quo, if you really want to leave a legacy. On the contrary, you can also decide to

maintain that miserable lifestyle by standing aloof without making any conscious effort to salvage the situation.

5. **Your adversaries plans, will come to pass**

Do you know the dreams of your adversaries? If no, then I will make it known to you. It is their optimum goal to see you in a deplorable situation, where their ultimate plans or strategies design for you, may come to pass. Even though you have all the needed tools at your disposal to prove them wrong, by going against all odds, the journey starts with action. Your decisive action can make the difference you are looking for. Bear in mind that, you can only prove them wrong with your positive actions that will obstruct them from executing their bogus plans.

Once you have seen the enormous benefit that comes with believing yourself, the onus now rest on you to wake up from your slumber and make that move. If you fail to decide early on, you will pay the price of not making that move later on. You will be deprived of the dreams and aspirations you have always dreamt of achieving. At first, it may seem impossible, but great things you thought could never happened, were plan and executed by ordinary people like you, before they became renowned.

If you really love your present condition, then nothing will urged you to strive for better goals. It takes a non-conformist mentality to change things in our community, our country and the world as a whole. When you start believing yourself, you will soon be noticed. Your self-believe will give you a sense of certainty to move from being coward to courageous, being timid to confidence and being nobody to somebody. At this stage in your life, you will realize that, making the move to believe yourself, was the best idea you have ever thought of doing. From that moment, you will acknowledge the fact that touching, feeling and experiencing greatness has not being an overnight achievement, but a calculated step to reach your goals, which started with just believe.

Believing alone will not be enough, until you put your believes into practice in order to experience greatness. The onus is on you, to take the initiative, you should have taken, when you were lacking self-believe. If you are waiting for the perfect time, to hit the ground running, may be that time will never come. Believing yourself does not mean that all that come your way will be rosy, but it will give you the positive attitude towards anything you set your mind on, as you quest to achieve greatness.

Once you believe yourself, if you pursue a goal and momentarily fail to get it right at the first instance, don't begin to fidget, for if nothing at all, you have learn ways that are not workable. In your second attempt, you will definitely avoid the plans that were not workable in your first plan. As you face any challenge with this mindset, the likelihood for you to triumph in your second attempt will be very high.

When you set the ball rolling, with some experiences from the first plan as coupled with yourself believe, you will definitely weather the storm without much stress, but if you fail, continue the cycle until you get it right. That is why believe is key, to the successful execution of any proposed ideas.

If you quit half way, due to frustrations and negative utterances coming from others, then you have permitted the insignificant views of others to dictate for you. If it happens like that, you will be force to relinquish your believe system and begin to pander to every whims of your adversaries. Even though they do not know much about your vision, you will later regret if, you realize how you have belittled yourself in such a weird manner, after seeing others achieving the things you said are impossible. Later in life, you will then curse your stars for not doing it.

Have you notice that believe, when altered by your adversaries can block your strategic plans and dump you where they precisely want you to be. That is why believing yourself, is crucial to the success of any individual. If your believing power is not well grounded, just a word or two from unscrupulous personalities can shut the dreams and aspirations you have nurtured over the years.

Food For Thought

As your confidence level shot up, you will realize the potentials you have. This will propel you to strive for growth mindset. Once you face life with these tools, no obstacles fashion against you will stand.

Henceforth, you will be a blessing to others as you rub shoulders with the elite in society. Believing yourself will help you to position your mind as you master courage to unravel the impediments that tend to block your path. This will pave the way for the greatness in you to begin.

So wake up from your slumber and ensure that, you put in your utmost best, by dealing with the problem directly. If you make the needed effort, by hitting the ground running, your believing power will take you places. By believing yourself, your steps, moves and words will be preceded by confidence.

Therefore, allay the fears in you, rise to your full height and draw from your self-believe, if you do, you will gradually achieve your desires, in the short possible time. When your desires come to fruition, the status quo in which you find yourself will always change in accordance with your vision. That is why, there is the need to believe yourself in order to experience great transformation, which will change your standard of living and make life better for you, in the ensuing years.

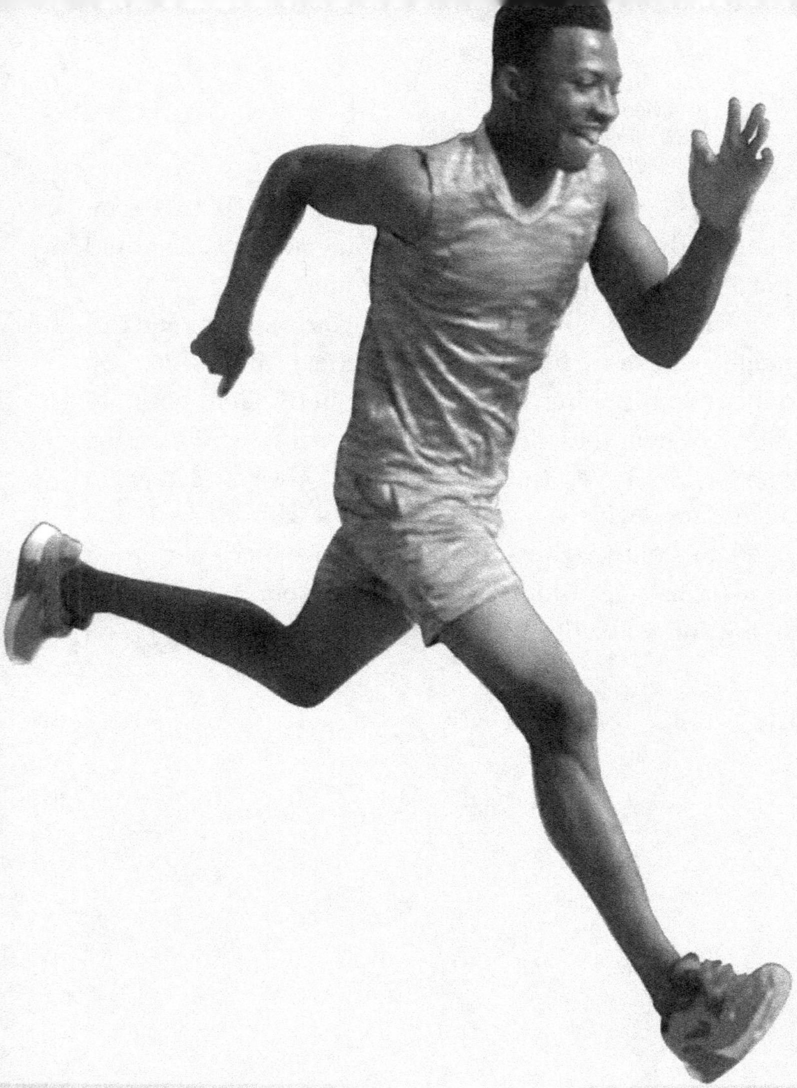

" **Your Strength Can Take You to Places, You Have Never Dreamt of Going**"

Richard Kyere-Boateng

CHAPTER TWO

Identify Your Strengths and Weaknesses

In order to believe yourself, you must first know your strengths and your weaknesses. This will stimulate you to know yourself. After making a clear distinction, between your strengths and your weaknesses, you will realize that, when challenges come your way, it can teach you an unforgettable lesson.

Do you know yourself as an individual? If yes, then you know your strengths and weaknesses. On the contrary, if you do not know yourself, then you need to know yourself. This is very essential since your positive attributes that are interpreted as your strength, can be highlighted to draw attention to a potential employer when applying for a job.

However, your negatives, which are mostly interpreted as your weaknesses, can be avoided, when applying for a job. If you realize the benefit that may come your way, when you turn your attention towards your strength at a tender age, it may certainly save you from years of struggling. It also lessens the time you will waste engaging in fruitless ventures, without making any headway. Therefore, I will entreat you to do whatever you can, in order to know yourself. If you do without hesitation, your strength can take you to places, you have never dreamt of going.

Below are few examples of weaknesses that people have, which I deem it relevant discussing it to help in our quest to reach great heights.

1. **Being synonymous with fear**

   Fear is the number one cause, of nervousness and insecurity that mostly cause an individual to fidget when delivering a speech, in an auditorium that is filled to capacity. Fear can discourage someone from pursuing his dreams and aspirations.

   When fear surrounds an individual, the abilities, skills and interests he/she has within, will gradually diminish. If it continues unabated, the individual will certainly lose the little courage left within him/her to finish a project. That is why in everything you do you must prepare your mind adequately to acquire the perseverance spirit in addition to self-believe, to face challenges head-on. If you do, fear will not have any ground to manoeuvre its way in all your endeavours. This can only happen, when you identify your weaknesses and deal with them.

   My dear friend, do you know that fear is in everyone? Therefore, if fear is your number one weakness, do not let your heart be troubled and completely give up on your dreams, just have a self-believe that you are not alone and you can climb all hurdles that come your way.

2. **Being synonymous with failure**

   Having a track record of failing, does not mean you will forever fail. Great people, who are often classified as, movers and shakers of society once fail. Therefore if you fail as a learner, remember you are not alone, thousands of individuals have fail already, hence, you will not be the first or last to taste the bitter pill of failure. Though is a bitter pill to swallow, in the long run, failure tends to provide experience to its target persons.

Do you know that failure is synonymous with great achievers? A typical example is the story of Thomas Edison; he failed several times in his quest of achieving greatness. Today his name is part of great people who defied the odds and came out with great ideas that have changed the status quo of the world, through his invention of light bulb.

Failure taught him several lessons that made him to discard all method that were not workable, until finally what was left became the workable method that made him a hero. How many failures have you discarded, keep on keeping on with the hard work, for one day, you won't discard what is left behind, since it will be the solution you have been longing for.

3. **Being synonymous with procrastination**

What you want to do must be done now, when you procrastinate, the probability to lose interest in pursuing your noble ideas may be very low. That is why believing yourself gives you the burning desire you need, to enable you pursue a course without hesitation. Believing yourself will free you from the shackles of procrastination and instil perseverance spirit in you.

In life, many people procrastinate because they think that, they are not worthy to carry out their

dreams. It all boils down to the fact that they lack self-believe, which could be attributed as their weaknesses. When you have an idea you want to implement, to help lessen a problem in your community, do not hesitate, just do it. Once you do, one day the impact will resonate with you, your community and beyond. When that time comes, your legacy will live on.

4. **Being entangled with opinion of others**

People do not believe in themselves because they think and believe that what others are saying about them is the optimum truth. For example, if someone relates them to an under achiever, who cannot achieve any positive things they set out to do in life, they accept that as reality and live with it for the rest of their lives.

You must not be oblivious to the fact that, some opinions are meant to encourage, uplift and urged you to press on, until you achieve the optimum. However, most opinions, spell doom for us. The negative once are often meant to put you in a state of complete disarray, where all the plans, ideas and initiatives you have, may die prematurely. So, be on the lookout and thread cautiously, to enable you reach your goals.

One thing you should know is that, before you make any significant progress in life, you must first deal with a weakness like fear, before huge gains can be made. Failure to do so, as you press ahead, fear can trap your effort and land your plan in a complete fiasco. This will drain you further and finally worsen your plight in the end.

5. Fear of public speaking

In order to overcome the fear of public speaking, an individual must make a conscious effort to follow the rudiments in public speaking. Once you practise constantly, the fear associated with public speaking, will soon reduce to its bare minimum. As a result, it may not pose any threat to you when delivering a speech in public. Do you know that, practice makes perfect? Once you practise, you will soon get the hang of it and move from being coward to courageous. At that moment, believes you have nurtured overtime, will help you speak with all the enthusiasm needed to enable you allay the fears that has entangle your life over the years and give you the charisma to speak confidently in your presentations.

6. Fear of starting a business

The fear of starting a new business can be alleviated by taking not just risk for starters, but a calculated risk, to enable you succeed in a grand style.

Remember, a calculated risk for start-ups will mostly place the business on a sound footing. Since, workable examples that have proven record may be employ to safeguard the young business from failing. Therefore, you must tread cautiously when venturing into a new business.

7. Fear of failing exams

Most often, there is the tendency for one to experience fear in exams after failing on several occasions. If you are afraid of failing again, do not worry because your

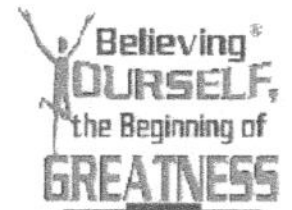

failure will be a thing of the past, but subject to paying a price, which most students see it as a serious hurdle. The prices include buying the right books, attending classes regularly and copying salient points during classes. Aside that, you can also, adopt the right learning strategies that resonates with your abilities.

Last but not least, if you can associate yourself with the brilliant students in class, you will be able to draw from their way of thinking, to help shape your personality. Once these are followed to the later, coupled with self-believe, the door of greatness will open soon.

Please, can you list your strength? Alternatively, maybe I will mention some of the positive signs that stimulate most people to believe themselves, so that you can at least follow them in your quest of achieving greatness. Below are few examples of positive attributes that people have, which are relevant to our discussion.

1. **The abilities you possess**

They are things you can offer, which normally comes natural. Abilities can often be equated to talent, which are mostly inborn skills that nature instils in people at birth that make them unique in certain way. If there are certain things that you can do with little effort, but look and sounds great to your peers without formal training in that aspect, then that is your abilities. Your abilities can be a powerful tool that will lead you to greatness.

If you can devote your time, money and effort to sharpen these potentials formally, your journey to greatness will hasten. So do not just identify your abilities and lazy around, without utilizing it. Hit the ground running with these abilities and you will soon reach your goals.

2. The skills you have

They can be learn or acquire through formal or informal education. In life, most skills you wish to acquire can be learn through formal or informal education. Remember that some skills are meant for a particular purpose and can also be transferred and utilized in other facet of life. You can sharping your skills through training.

When people, bombard you with negative thoughts, do not stand aloof and waste your precious moments, pondering over these debilitating messages, which can limit your way of thinking. So let it go by channelling your free time, to acquire learnable skills that can help you turn the impossibilities people see in you, to possibilities. If you sharpen these skills, you will be able to combat most challenges that may come your way.

Most skills are design to solve specific problems, so take note and channelled these skills, to suit your purpose in life. If you do it without hesitating, you will accomplish your dreams and aspirations in no time, since your skills will enable you execute your work in a skilful way.

3. The interest that drives you

They are the things you are passionate about that you often do because you love it. An interest can be equated to your hobby, which at times brings you joy

and fulfilment. Interest is very essential when pursuing a course or applying for a job. If you make an effort and follow your interest, you will never fall prey to negative utterances, because once you come across them in your line of duty, your interest will keep you at bay.

These three thematic areas if carefully analysed to the best of your abilities, can spark your interest to believe yourself, which will gradually lead you to greatness. After knowing your strength and weaknesses, it would be prudent to focus on your strength. In order to known your strength, you must first identify several words that others easily associate you with, when it comes to life. Words like hardworking, reliable, faithful, noble, diligent, efficient, dedicated, jovial, confident, meticulous, intuitive and sympathetic can speaks volumes of a person's character.

When some of these words are equated to you as your true character, it can easily give a clue to anyone who cares to know your strength. After listing all the points that make up your strength, you can now make those core areas, as your focal point. If you do, you may easily strategize around these thematic areas. If you are still not certain about the realities of your strength, you can check out these extra clues, it may draw your attention to things that can possibly direct you in your quest to discover all your hidden strengths. As you strive hard to reach great heights in the short possible time, take note of the discussion below, to help you toe the line of greatness. These are as follows:

1. **What do your friends like about you?**

Do you have sweet voice? When you sing, do people always, praise you? If yes, then singing or sweet voice can be a powerful tool that you can highlight as your strength, as and when the need arises.

If you are smart enough, you can align it with your career and once you do without hesitation, it can lead to the beginning of greatness in your life. In life, if you do what you love and your friends admired, gradually it will capture the attention of others and subsequently boost your confidence level. If you continue each day, it will inspire you to believe yourself.

2. **What usually burns your heart, when you see it happening?**

It may happen that God has given you the needed strength to map up strategies to combat these anomalies that irritates your life. If you can carefully, analysed yourself you will notice that, solutions to these anomalies are within your reach. Once you focus your mind on solving them, it can leads to self-confidence and further urge you to believe yourself. For instance, if you see people in trouble and empathize with them even though you do not know them, then it is telling you, that you are caring, these can be highlighted as your strength when applying for any job that requires that attribute.

3. **Focus on your natural abilities**

When you direct your attention towards things you can do with ease, you will soon be an expert in that area of study. By focusing on abilities of yours, significant impact can be made with just a little effort, which can gradually lead you to greatness. You can do

so, by paying close attention to your strength with regard to certain capacities such as; the skills, talents and the passion you have in pursuing your set objectives. By so doing, your interest, skills and inborn talent, can draw you closer to achieving greatness.

If you make a conscious effort to focus on your strength, the benefits that you will derive are enormous. Therefore, get your act together and forge ahead in order to reach your goals and aspirations.

Let us look at some of the benefits discussed below and acquaint ourselves with it as we journey to the land of greatness. In the wake of negativity, individuals can focus on their strength to stand the test of time. Once you are aware of your strength, it will motivate you to face life head on.

1. **You will achieve your goals**

You will soon reach your goals, once you start focusing your mind on your strength, if not for anything, you may realize the positive attributes you possess and utilized it judiciously, to attain your goals. When you come to terms with the fact that your life is in a mess and make effort to change your present condition, you will be able to build confidence that will drive home your dream, with all the zeal it deserved. Whereas your colleague, who often delve deep into the negative side of life and apportion blame, will be left behind.

As you journey to the land of your dreams, with all the enthusiasm it deserves, the pendulum at a point in time, may swing from good to bad. Things may be harder, tougher and unbearable. When that time comes, your focusing mind that takes cognizance of your strength will see you through the moment of heat that may come your way, as you dare to achieve the optimum. If you are able to draw from your strength, you may acquire all the positive character traits embedded within you. Your strength may guide you as you plan, implement and evaluate these issues in your quest of achieving greatness.

Therefore, I will entreat you to focus your attention on your strength to help you attain victory in the end.

2. You will be less influence by negative minds

When you focus your mind on greatness, with tools like self-believe and perseverance, it will create a strong positive shield around you. This will reduce the influence that negative minds have upon your life.

When comment starts coming from various angles, which are primarily set out to demoralized you, the shield you have set around you early on, will give you the needed strength to withstand any good for nothing words that your adversaries persuade you to believe.

As you focus your mind on your strength to reach a higher pedestal, it will be very easy to draw distinctions between the good, the bad and the ugly things that come your way.

Since your strength can give you the power to select the best option, when the time comes, let your strength be the driving power that may lead you to the path of greatness, as you soldier on in life.

3. Others will emulate your lifestyle

Within your community and beyond, the youth who have been seeing the sort of impact you are making, will begin to emulate your lifestyle, by drawing from your persona to reach the top. When such time comes, you can reflect upon the inspiration that emanates from your strength to help motivate those who need such advice genuinely.

As others imitate you, they will inform their friends with regard to the lives you are touching and the impact you are making. This will soon make you a renowned personality in your own small way as you move along to the top.

All these can easily manifest itself, if you can tilt your focus towards your strength and begin to believe yourself as you match towards greatness. The believing attitude, will equip you with all the zeal you need in order to live an exemplary life that is worth pursuing.

4. You will cherish your personality

When others are focusing their minds on their weaknesses, while seeing themselves as nothing, you will gather momentum and press on until you reach new heights.

Through self-believe, your personal development will grow from strength to strength. Due to the potentials you have identified within you, there would not be any cause for alarm, when others try to frustrate your vision with negative utterances.

Once you cherish your persona, you will be in full flow as your confidence shot up in every speech, presentation or messages you deliver.

5. **You will release the stress associated with your weakness**

Once you identify your strength and stay glued to it, there is no way that, your mind will be thinking mostly about your weaknesses, since your strength will occupy your mind and relieve you of the stress that are often associated with your weaknesses.

When these stresses are released, you will get the freedom to dissect issues relating to your desires and aspirations with an open-mind. This mindset will be devoid of any blemished that will force you to relinquish your dreams and aspirations.

Aside that, it will stimulate you to pursue your goals with your strength in mind, to enable you achieve them within a short possible time.

You will do yourself a great honour, when you take time to identify your strengths and weaknesses. This is the easiest part of the research, once you identify these traits, it will be the starting point in your quest of focusing on your strength. After discovering your strength and weaknesses, if you do not make any effort to focus on your strength and get the best out of it, you may not see major changes in your life.

What matters most, is what you do after discovering this two contrasting character traits of yours. You will make a huge difference in your life, when you take a solitary walk to greatness, by considering your strengths and weaknesses while focusing primarily on your strength to see your dream through.

Food For Thought

If you focus on your strengths and put behind you, your weaknesses, it will help you in your journey to greatness. Remember your weaknesses have nothing good to offer you except agony, depression and regret. Spending precious moments pondering over your weaknesses, will only draw you back.

On the contrary, your strength offers you, confidence, positive mindset and greatness. Therefore reaching the top depends on how you manage your weaknesses such as fear, failure, procrastination and indecision. If this is done, you can now focus on your abilities, skills and interest to bring your ideas to life. This can easily happen if you can make good use of your self-confidence and clear all the self-doubt you have nurtured over time, the ideas you have been grooming for years will come to fruition.

For your information, you have been focusing too much on others abilities, skills, interests and success, at the expense of your own. Don't get carried away by the achievements of others and forget to work on your dreams. I will urge you not to look beyond yourself, but look within you and you will soon discover some unique resources your maker has endowed you with, for instance, your abilities and interest. I will entreat you to wake up from your slumber, take charge of your life and putting into action the ideas, skills and interest instilled within you. If you continue to do this, your tremendous dream will see the light of day.

Don't act like a defeatist, when myriad of challenges meet you half way, into any project you are embarking on. For the defeatist, they do not always expect you to succeed in anything you set your mind on, since they loosely give in to failure without thinking otherwise. That is why it would be prudent on your part to focus on your strengths and leave behind you your weaknesses, to enable you reach your goals and aspirations with ease.

"Your Mental Breakthrough
Can Easily Happen,
When You Have the Guts to Turn
Negative Opinions to Positive"
Richard Kyere-Boateng
Believing YOURSELF, the Beginning of GREATNESS

CHAPTER THREE

Turning Negative Opinions to Positive

Once you have identified your strengths and weaknesses, the onus rest on you to focus your attention on how your weaknesses, negativities and obstacles can be turn to positive. If you are able to achieve this, it can galvanize you into action, as you long for greatness. This will urge you to press on, once you ignore, eliminate or turn negative opinions to positive. This is necessary because, the consequences of negative thought can terrify you, in all your endeavours, as you face life head-on, in your daily pursuit.

Negative thoughts have the tendency to drain you both physically and psychologically, hence the need to turn negative thought that surrounds your life to positive. People who believe in themselves mostly, have the ability to turn various negative thoughts they encounter every day, to positive thoughts.

When you allow negative thought to overshadow your life, it is like digging your own grave, when it becomes severe, you will need a conscious effort and a divine intervention to overcome it. I can say without equivocation that, negative thought creates internal struggling within an individual that can kill the person slowly, without him/her knowing it.

If you cannot ignore the negative thoughts, you can control how you react to it. Let me chip in my lifetime testimony that I encountered so many years ago. When I

was a teenager, there was a time in my life where negativity engulfed me like a flame of fire, which took over my words, actions and emotions, my thinking ability became low, life was nothing but a pain in the heart. There were dozens of negative questions that befell me during these trying times. It took the timely intervention of several inspirational and motivational words that distanced me from the servitude of negativity. Aside that, reading of the scriptures, listening to sermons and lessons learnt from others, gave me the power to face life head-on.

There is always a way out, as you battle with negative thinking. There is a strong possibility of leaving the servitude of negativity. Negative thought however, breeds negative emotions that often leave indelible mark on your mind that manifest itself in your words, actions and emotions. At this stage, when others begin to see how your inability to turn negative opinions to positive statement is having a rippling effect on your life, they will then associate you with negativity.

Do you often question the status quo, when it comes to life? If yes, then why is it that, negativity often dominates your thoughts, actions and emotions, instead of positivity? Well if you make a critical analysis of the words you say, the emotional sentiments that go through your mind and the various actions you mostly take in life, you will notice that, your thoughts influence your emotions while your emotions influence your actions. In reality, your thought starts the baton and hand it over to your emotion, your emotion pass the baton to your action, your action then finish your mission by causing things to happen. The result may be good or bad, depending on the thought initiated at the beginning. The process goes on, any time you cause things to happen. That is why, you should be mindful of things that go through your mind and the emotional sentiments that triggers your action, must be carefully scrutinized to avert series of mishaps.

As you crave for positive mindset, it will be prudent to change these good for nothing statements, into positive Statements. In most cases, your mental breakthrough can easily happen, when you have the guts to turn negative opinions to positive. This can be achieved by letting it go of negative utterances that restrain your life, by pulling yourself together and putting into practice, these steps:

1. **Be around positive people**

    When negativity engulfs you, at that particular moment, just surround yourself with positive minded people. As they interact with you within this positive environment, their words will neutralize all negative utterances that have engulf you and replace it with inspiring, motivational and thought-provoking statements. Once you encounter these encouraging words, it may change your mood and motivate you to persevere until you reach your goals.

    Above all, their constructive criticisms, may serve as a guiding principle, which will finally trigger the positive thoughts you are longing for. This may gradually lead you to your goals and aspirations. So, never hesitate to mingle with positive minds when negative words occupy your mind.

2. **Sing in order to build your self-esteem**

    When you are saddle with negative thoughts so much that it is taking over your thoughts, this solution may

be of help to you. You can sing a joyous, motivational and inspirational song to release it. Singing can turn your emotions or state of mind around, from negative either to positive or vice versa. Through singing, you may also achieve the positive aspect of your emotions that can revive you. If you can take advantage of singing as a tool, it can equip you against any negative tendencies that may serve as an obstacle in your journey to greatness.

Below are three reasons why, you have to sing when you suddenly meet negativity, in your pursuance of greatness.

i. **You can sing to tell your own story**

When others are trying to fabricate a story for you as they influence your mind through their negative words, actions and emotions, do not let your heart be troubled. One thing you should know is that, their main objective is to kill your spirit by altering the ideas, strength and enthusiasm that has shaped yourself esteem up until now.

Once you put your words into singing, you will be able to deal with the issues and the negative tag that people have associated your name with will neutralized. Soon and very soon these negative utterances will no longer have an adverse effect on you, because the song that you will sing, will finally relieved you off the stress associated with negativity and give you the right lyrics that will motivate you within, in your quest to reach greatness.

ii. **You can sing to create identity for yourself**

Through singing, people can identify you with, either negativity or positivity. It all boils down to the ability for you to select a song that contains the right lyrics, which can release you from the excruciating, pain of negativity. Whenever negative thought entangles your life, singing can help alleviate the challenges it poses to you, if you can make it a routine.

iii. **Your mood, emotions and energy can be enhanced through singing**

This can break the shackles of negativity that entangles your life. As a result, it will reduce the stress that often occurs to you, due to negativity. When you sing continuously, your behaviour can change from the act of lazing around, to being conscious about what is happening around you, since you will be on the lookout, in your quest of reaching your goals.

If the lyrics of the song are packed with positive, inspiring and motivational words, it can easily swing your mind from negative feeling to positive feeling. These positive vibes, emanating from the lyrics of your song, can be a stimulant that will lead you to greatness.

3. **Avoid jumping into conclusion**

To avoid the probability of jumping into conclusion, you must try to concentrate on facts and noticeable events. Through this, you may notice that, at times, what you see and hear can be false. Therefore,

jumping into conclusion without probing into issues or personalities at stick can be detrimental.

In life, jumping into conclusion has landed innocent lives in prison, at the hospital and others in their grave. That is why you must gather enough information before levelling accusation against innocent people. Instant justice, like mob attack that often leads to the killing of innocent lives can easily be averted if issues resulting in the attack were thoroughly investigated before the unpardonable act. However, most often third parties dictate the pace for the masses and together, they perpetrate the reprehensible act with impunity.

Most often than not, you may seem to forget that, many people learn each day, adapt to new situations and change their behaviour. Therefore, the personality you knew some days ago may not be the same personality now. Sometimes, if you are uncertain about something, the propensity to jump into conclusion is very high. You may be oblivious to the fact that truth only arises from correct analyses, so to avoid negative thought always avoid the tendency of jumping into conclusion. This always happens because you do not look at things from the holistic perspective.

Nevertheless, you rather conclude when you have little or no information. Most often accusation may be flying around, when such time comes do not conclude until you have enough proof to buttress your curiosity. I will urge you not to be too judgmental based on your instincts alone especially, when you do not have enough facts. This is what great people hate doing because, being judgmental means, you are closing a window of opportunity to solving the problem since there is always a solution to a problem if you approach it with an open-mind.

Creative and innovative personalities are of the view that, being judgmental at the initial stages of your quest to creating something new, can obstructs the ability to stretch your imaginations. Therefore, you must train your mind to enable you substantiate the truth in most conversations you have with others. In life, there are two sides to the same coin, as a result, we can mostly get hold of the truth out of any interaction, if we can curiously analyse the issues from both angles. Once you listen to both sides, the truth will surface at the right time. This will help you in your quest to ascertain the fact yourself, without relying on third parties.

For the most part of our life, statements from third parties may be true or false. Owing to the fact that, some people may fabricate stories about their colleagues that have no bases in order to win favours from their superiors. This barbaric act of theirs, may throw their colleague's life into disarray. That is why you need to give it a benefit of doubt by listening to the other side of a story before judging anyone. Who knows, you may be allowing information from third parties, which may not be the complete truth, to dominate your mind and kill your creative abilities. If you do not follow these guidelines, most often, there will be a pain in the heart, which has no bases.

In life is good to give everyone the benefit of doubt, by listening to them without any prejudice, this

will allow you, to treat them, the way you see them, not how others, perceive them. I will entreat you not to fall prey to gossips, because most of the prejudice you have with regard to other personalities, are often based on gossips.

Before you set the tone to gossip, step back and take a sober reflection by putting yourself in that person's shoes, if you do, you will realize that, it is not easy to be in one's shoe. You will then take a quick detour and now begin to empathize with the person, especially when the problem resonates with your life, rather than gossiping about the person. That is why you must reflect on the utterances of the personality under discussion, since assumptions always bring hasten decision, which may not be the right decision.

Most at times, we do not take time to gather enough information on a personality, before passing our final comment. If you take time to gather enough fact, you will come to realization that, some of the comments you have always been passing about others will stop, because it may not be the truth.

How to avoid jumping into conclusions, when confronted with delicate issues that demand deep thinking, if you follow the instruction below, it will let you gather enough fact before passing your final comment. Below are the do's and don'ts.

i. **Accept uncertainty**

This will help you clear your mind from any predefine ideas. Accepting uncertainty will mostly allow you to tackle issues with an open-mind before making a distinct choice. On the other hand, it will let you gather enough information, before making the final decision.

ii. **Don't predict until you have enough fact**

It would be prudent to have enough information, relating to an issue at stake, before finally analysing the issue and arriving at a decision, when problems crop up. The crux of the matter is that enough information can let you do due diligence to issues, before you finally make the move to predict the outcome.

iii. **Don't give chance to only one possibility, but consider other options**

To avoid jumping into conclusion, do not rely on only one option or possibility since there is always, two sides of the same coin. So after listening to one side of any story, do not jump into conclusion without listening to the other side of the story.

Most often, when people are entangled with problems they have encountered with others, they mostly narrate their story to suit their personal interest. In some cases, their choice of words, actions and emotions will easily convince you to pander to their whims and caprices. Hence, I will not be surprise if you have ever fall for the antics of a person in trouble, who had issues with someone, because you did not delved deep into the issues under discussion before judging it. In reality you may have listen to only one side of the story and being oblivious to the other side, but you still went ahead to judge. Later in life, you

may regret an impulsive decision you have made when the complete truth comes out.

Therefore, I will entreat you to tread cautiously when making decisions and always look before you leap, else you may quickly move to defend someone who in reality, may not warrant your attention.

iv. **Probe into issues by interrogating them**

Do not accept the norm, probe into issues as and when they crop up, by asking questions like, how, when, and why. It will push the person you are interrogating, to open up the discussion, by revealing several instances that occurred, which will further lead you to discover some hidden details that will help you to uncover information that the person doesn't what to reveal. Questions that are thought-provoking, will always urge someone to come out with the truth without knowing it.

v. **Stay totally independent as much as you can, when discussing issues**

The more you stay independent of the opinions of others, it will urge you to stay resolute, focus your attention on the issues at stick and be less influence by what others think of you.

For the most part of your life, it will give you the opportunity to associate yourself with most of the relevant issues that may help promote your agenda. This can only work if you have inner motivation that will replace the views of others and keep you company when loneliness, dullness and fatigue set in. In the end, if you are able to

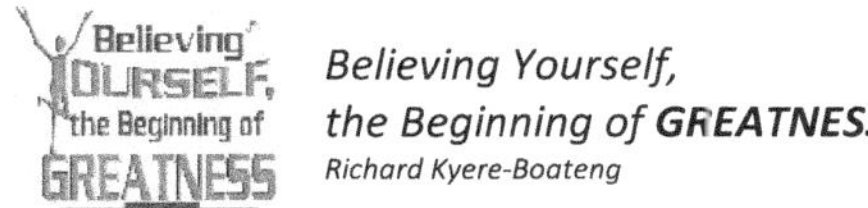

restrain yourself from the negative opinions of others, jumping into conclusion will be a thing of the past. Henceforth, you will not be swayed by the opinionated views of your opponents that will geared you towards the servitude of negativity.

vi. **Don't take things personal**

Do not always personalize issues when you come across them. At times, the issues under discussions may not be related to you directly, but it may be a general issue, which needs general approach.

Once you personalized it, the conclusion at the end of the analysis, will not augur well during decision making, since you are likely to follow your emotions rather than, facts on the ground to arrive at a decision. If you personalize issues, it may often give room for emotional sentiments, parochial interest and self-glorification. When every issue is personalized, it may not give you an open mind to tackle issues but give rise to closed minds, which may affect your final decision.

4. **Worrying about unimportant things**

In life many people worry unnecessarily, why am I saying this? They spent most of their time thinking about issues, which has no relevance in their quest of achieving greatness.

Do you know that, there is more to life than just mere worries? Are you also aware of the consequences associated with worries? Worrying unnecessary can lead to a serious pain in the heart of

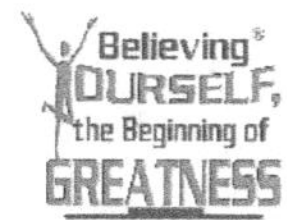

someone that may have a long-term effect on his/her life.

At times, worrying about unnecessary things, can lead to emotional instability and cause someone to loose trust in themselves and gradually lead to low self-esteem. One thing you must know is that, your assumptions produce who you are and what you can achieve. Instead of worrying about these little hiccups, you can channel your effort in finding ways of solving the menace.

5. Avoid been pessimistic

For the pessimist, they know nothing, but always see gloomy pictures, even in the midst of hope. When there is a green light, giving us clues that things will be better, they will still be focusing on negativity. This happens because, they do not possess any positive vibes, due to that, their words, actions and emotions are always geared towards impossibility.

Therefore, in your quest of achieving greatness, you must always avoid moving or associating yourself with the pessimist. Refusal to do so, the light that you are dreaming to see at the end of the tunnel, you will be forced to believe that is doom.

6. Let your small achievement lit your light

Occupy your mind with the small or little gains you have accomplished, in your challenging moment, when hurdles become difficult to climb, your small gains can urge you on. If you have achieved something small before, it will always give you the needed impetus to soldier on to achieve the biggest, in the near future.

The experience you have accrued in achieving small gains, may pave the way for greater achievements, later in life. So, just be consistent and break complex problems into smaller segments that can be dealt with, as each day go by. In life, progress can easily be made, when you tackle issues bit by bit, there may be a significant progress in your quest of solving the issue at stick. When you focus your attention in achieving smaller gains, your life will be full of greater gains as you walk through life.

7. **Always give yourself the opportunity to try again**

Self-doubt will always crop up, in the midst of anything that one craves to achieve. Once it surfaces, it will always paint a mental picture that going ahead to achieve the impossibility is not possible. One basic thing that makes the extra-ordinary people different from others is their ability to manage negativity. Trying again gives you the ability to advance your plans to enable you know what will work and what will not work.

In the same vein, several great projects of your generation, suffered failure during the planning stage, when these dreams were still under consideration, but with a second thought, perseverance and opportunity to try again, pushed it to the implementation and supervisory stages. So if, you have fail, do not throw up your hands in despair, but try again and you will be closer to your dreams.

What matters most, is for you to realize that you need a second chance in order to make amends towards what you failed to achieve. The second approach often comes which much experience as compared to the first attempt. Hence, never give up on your dreams, allow yourself to face the challenge once again and you will never regret doing it.

8. Be confident and trust your instincts

Whenever, you are stuck in a project, because of your inability to achieve your set objective, do not lose your confidence, but trust your instinct and give yourself, another opportunity to try again. Always remember the popular saying that, winners do not quit and quitters never win.

After weighing all your strength and ideas and still, no concrete progress has been made, in each challenge, you can then count on your instincts. They are gestures that, shield us from danger and insincere attitude that prompt us to make a decision or choice base on our inner feeling. When you trust your instincts, no matter the negative comments you may encounter, you will have the confidence that, you can weather the storm.

The crux of the matter is that, is not the volume of negativity that engulf you, which can make or break you in life, but the ability to turn these negative influence into positive feelings that matters most in your journey to greatness. This will rejuvenate us to believe in ourselves thereby given us the power to turn them to positives. Your instincts sometimes, give you cues of what someone really means not his/her choice of words. Whereas, non-verbal cues also give you a gist of what is going through a person's mind not necessary his/her choice of words.

Your confidence will boost your morale and urge you to soldier on even, when things are not working well for you. When you trust your instincts, it will mostly give you the power to believe yourself, as you battle your way out through the storms of life, your instincts can serve as a guiding angel that can direct your path to achieving the impossibilities in life.

9. **Preoccupied your mind with the bigger picture**

Before you begin any project, always picture the results and its benefit in your mind. Certainly, it will provide you with a robust energy to battle any comments and criticisms that are meant to deter you from reaching your goals.

If you allow the results of the project to influence your thoughts, actions and emotions, negative words will come and go without living any harmful effect on your life. When others are wishing the down fall of the project, the bigger picture you have in mind, will equipped you with the perseverance spirit to press on, until you reach your ultimate goal.

10. **Have a winner mindset**

People with winning mentality, have one thing in common, they often refuse to bow to pressures from drainers that, are meant to lure them to stop focusing on their dreams and aspirations. If you bow to the enticing opinions of these detractors, you will end up spelling doom for yourself. That is why, it is good to

know the way of thinking of drainers and the strategies they used when attacking their victim. Once you know, it will give you an upper hand against them. Before they launch any attack, the winner mindset you possess, will give you the power to withstand them, while you forge ahead to attain greatness.

11. Develop a resilient, unyielding and amazing strategy to combat negative minds

As days go by, negative minds will always confront you in any activity you pursue, whether you like it or not. They will bang into your life in your quest of making a purposeful move in life. If you allow them room to explore your thought and dictate your actions and inactions, they will tell you several reasons why, your plan will fail.

The enticing offers of the negative mind may lure you gradually until you finally compromise your plan and accept the alternative they will offer you in the long run. In most cases, the offers they will provide may glitter, but bear in mind that all that glitters is not gold. Therefore, wise up and develop ways that will help you prepare your mind in a way that you will not succumbed to pressures from negative minds. Once you do, their negative influence will change your positive vibes.

Turning negative opinions into positive opinions demand a vigorous effort, coupled with a rigorous approach to be able to attain this goal. The people you know in your community and your social circles, in most cases, want you to think and act like them. The moment you try to act in a manner that seems like you are making headway in life, it will often give them the cause to pounce on you with all the negative words they can think of, just to belittle your effort.

Once you realize that, you have a purpose in life, do not pander to the whims of a negative mind and be a looser when brilliant ideas are going through your mind. Lions do not wait for elephants to dictate the pace of their movement. They call the shot, whenever they feel like doing so, since a lion believe that it is the king of the jungle. This mindset, mostly distinguish the lion from other gigantic wild animals such as the elephant, hippopotamus and several animals, who could have merit the attribute of the king in the jungle but their mentality limit their actions. You are also a king in your own small way, so why should you allow the insignificant words uttered by some unscrupulous persons, truncate your lifetime dreams. Imbibe the tenets of the lion by believing yourself and very soon, you will swiftly lead in every activity you embark on.

So, wake up from your slumber, heed to your intuition, avoid the defeatist, and take a solitary walk to greatness. Your perseverance spirit will sweep away every vestige of negativity and clear your path as you quest for greatness.

Hence, as you move along the path to greatness, do not expect encouragement from everyone you come across, be inspired by your positive attributes since the motivational power you are looking for is within you, put it to test and you will be a victor. When the way seems bleak and tough to continue, remember to keep walking with all the ideas and dreams you have in mind until you reach your goals. The tough days you are seeing today will soon be a thing of the pass, if only you will persevere and stay focus within

the confines of your dreams, sooner rather than later, you will reach great heights.

For how long will you put your destiny in the hands of someone who lack vision and have no plans of attaining greatness. Wise up and let this catchphrase be your guiding principle, birds of a feather flock together. If you associate yourself with people who are not going anywhere, the possibility of reaching nowhere is very high. In the same vein, if you move with likeminded persons, who have similar goes and aspirations, the influence they will make in your life, will help you reach your goals without qualms.

I will entreat you to try as much as you can and put behind you, negative comments that emanates from the pessimist. Once you do, their utterances will not have any ramifications on your life.

Food For Thought

> The road to greatness is full of challenges, but most of these challenges are often triggered by negative opinions and the choices you make. Therefore, having the power to turn negative opinions to positive, can give you the needed resistance, to fight against any oppressive force that may obstruct your actions. If you can ignore, eliminate or turn negative opinions to positive, you will be able to face life head on. With a winning mindset, you will see negative statement as a challenge that one has to surmount, before a bigger impact can be attained. If you put it into practise, greatness will be nearer to you than you ever thought.
>
> Therefore, I will entreat you to get your act together and devise a way of managing negativity effectively. When this is done, you will reach your goals and

aspirations as scheduled without delay. Aside that, you must be remarkably resilient, to withstand the antics of negative personalities and be a top-notch that your adversaries will struggle to crack. They will try hard to obstruct your plans, but finally they may come to realization that, they have tried all these years to obstruct your dreams, but to no avail.

If you continue to hold fast to the principles of turning negative opinions to positive preserved in this book, your opinionated friends may one day, through their hands in the air in despair. This may happen due to your unstoppable, relentless and unyielding character traits you have nurtured overtime, which may give your detractors, sleepless night.

I will urged you to do all you can, to acquire the skills in turning negative ideas that you come across to positive. Once this is done, you may trample over any obstacle that will come your way and finally reach your goals and aspirations with ease.

"Your Discerning Mind Can Help You Figure Out, the Truth in Most Situations"
Richard Kyere-Boateng
Believing YOURSELF, the Beginning of GREATNESS

CHAPTER FOUR

Having a Discerning Mind

In order to believe yourself, you will need the required wisdom and understanding to sift through information that may come your way. This is very crucial because, is not every information you come across that will be of benefit to you. At times, some information may require wisdom and understanding for you to evaluate them and select the relevant ones that can encourage, energize and trigger your intuition to believe yourself.

Life is full of myriad of choices, which can place you in a state of confusion, when the time comes for you to make a critical choice out of similar options. Your discerning mind can help you figure out, the truth in most situations. For instance, one must be able to draw a line between good and bad decision, negative and positive opinions, fake and original products and truth and lies in a message. Other choices include a right partner and a gold digger, friends and enemies you come across.

Henceforth, when the time comes to make that decision, lean on your discerning mind to enable you, discern in the right direction. At times two distinct options, which can easily be identified as two different things, are package in a way that makes them lookalike. For instance, fake and original products may share similar attributes that makes it difficult to distinguish between them. In most cases, if a person does not have discerning mind, it may be

difficult for him or her to differentiate between truth and lies. Most often, regardless of your educational background, age, sex, colour and geographical location, if you do not have a discerning mind most of the decisions you will take, may not augur well for you in life.

When you lack a discerning mind that can let you delved deep into issues to uncover the authenticity of it, fraudsters can easily dupe you. Sometimes, some of the things that can aid you to distinguish between similar things are mostly shrouded in secrecy. It will take a discerning mind to sift through and discover the shortcomings in any situation before making right uncompromising choice.

For the most part of our daily lives, the conversation we always have, some of our utterances are meant to encourage, others are to flatter, whereas few of them are meant to demotivate and finally kill your inner feelings and believes. That is why you need to know, and develop your discretional abilities, in order to read between the lines and be able to put them at their various categories.

After categorizing these ideas, you can now select the ones that suit your needs as you toe the line of greatness. When you get the opportunity to discuss any issue of great importance with someone, tools like emotional intelligence, discretion, compassion, diligence and courtesy can be employed to help get the best out of any conversation that comes your way.

Below are steps to consider when exercising discerning mind as you interact with people. It will let you sift through issues before making tough and uncompromising decision.

1. **Create enabling environment to start the conversation**

An enabling environment can be created when an individual begins a conversation with an open mind. This can help build trust in the person you are interacting with, in order to acquire important information you will need during the discussion. As you listen with rapt attention, the listener will also begin to trust your judgment. This will let the conversation flow without any hindrance. When the conversation continue unabated, basic information needed, to make your interaction successful, will be disclosed by the person whom, you are interacting with, due to the trust you have built at the beginning.

Once an enabling environment has been established, the tendency for you to acquire the information you are looking for will be easier, since there will be enough room for freedom of expression, which will allow both persons to share ideas and feeling without any prejudice. This will break all barriers and allow the discussion to go on without partiality. The conducive environment created, will finally aid you to ascertain the truth through the spirit of discernment.

2. **Determine the right moment to respond to a conversation or ask questions**

As you interact with someone, throughout your conversation, you must know when to chip in certain information and when not to do so. This can be done effectively, if your discerning mind prompts you to

respond adequately to issues under discussion at the right time.

If you follow the conversation, you will be clear on when a certain response is needed and when the best option is silent. At that particular moment, your discerning mind can be employ to enable you respond adequately, as and when they need arises. This will allow the one you are interacting with, have the notion that, you are a good listener and love sharing what you have. As a result, the discussion will go on and on, until the topic under discussion, is completely exhausted.

3. **Choose the right word at the right time**

Words may be offensive, archaic, formal, informal, jargon, just to mention a few. I will entreat you to be mindful of the words you choose when discussing an issue with others, in order not to hurt the feelings of people you interact with in your daily encounter.

When you interact with someone, the age, sex, religious believes, educational background and their cultural setting can pre-inform you on certain specific words to use and the ones you need not to use. As the conversation begins, the analysis will then follow suit at any giving stage, which will then help you to get the best out of every conversation.

Once, the right word take its rightful position in a conversation, the interaction you are having will flow smoothly without any difficulties. By using the right word at the right time, the person you are interacting with will finally feel at home. As a result, you will definitely get the best out of the conversation, since your counterpart will be willing to respond adequately to your submissions.

4. Be mindful of your body language

There is a saying that actions speaks louder than words, therefore you must always, relate your actions with your words, to enable others believe in you, during discussions. If your actions are in line with your words, a discerning mind, will notice it during the discussion.

On the contrary, if your actions are in contrast to your words, people who are interacting with you will notice the insincerity in your utterances. After critical observation of your utterances, they may decide not to disclose some information to you. When this happens, you will not be aware of some vital information needed to make an informed decision, when the need arises.

5. Disguise your emotional sentiments

Sometimes it is good to hide your emotions. This will allow you to tackle issues objectively, without revealing your emotional sentiments.

When issues are tackled with your emotions, it does not often give you the opportunity to face facts as it is, since your emotions will often take centre stage in most of your decisions. Your emotions, will now dominate the decisions you will make, without assessing the issues at stick. Once the issues at stick, is not the premise upon which judgement is made, the probability to deviate from the issues, will be very high.

The benefits of using your discerning mind

Discerning mind when used judiciously before, during and after a conversation can help you acquire, the better side of any interaction you encounter with others each day, as you battle with life. When you make a conscious effort to believe yourself, discerning mind will come to you naturally. Once you believe in your own decision, your confidence level in making decisions will shot up. Below are some of the benefits of using your discerning mind.

1. **You can easily ascertain the truth**

   Through discerning mind, you will be able to discover the truth, in a discussion, after series of discussions. This happens, when you make good use of your discerning power to analyse issues and make an informed decision. This will let you sift through issues and select the best. All these can easily be achieved by first believing yourself. After that, it will give you the power to step into the world of confidence and be able to ascertain the truth in most situations. Therefore, I will urge you to move heaven and earth to acquire this tool to enable you analyse issues without much difficulty.

2. **You can easily ignore irrelevant information**

   When you delved into issues as they crop up, your discerning mind can manifest itself through self-believe. It will give you the wisdom to discern on various information and ignore the irrelevant ones, which does not have any bearing in one's life, during discussion, as issues on fold. Through discernment, information can be filtered at source to ensure that, only the relevant ones are captured. When the right information is gathered, it will be easy to recall it when the need arises, due to the concise nature of the information.

3. You will gain a psychological urge over your counterpart

When the opportunity comes for you to interact with a friend, colleague or a client, once you make the move to interact, you will always be psychologically prepared, before the conversation begin. During the conversation, you will look for clues that will assist you to way options, before making an informed decision.

When the conversation begins, you may have a psychological advantage over them, due to the discerning mind you possess. Your facial expressions, choice of words and signals from your instinct will give you the support you need, to stay composed until the conversation ends.

4. It enables you to look at issues in a holistic manner

People, with discerning mind, often tackle issues holistically, before drawing conclusion. This often guides them to make the right decision, by studying issues to the best of their knowledge, and critically analysing each side of the issue before finally, reaching a decision. When all aspect surrounding a problem is carefully scrutinized, the tendency for you to make the right decision that may lead you gradually to greatness will be high.

5. It gives you the wisdom to discern on issues

Before proper analysis can be achieved in any challenging situation, discerning minds often play a major role in your quest of reaching the right decision. That is why, believing yourself can help in nurturing your mind, to acquire the discerning power that will assist you, when it comes to decision making. By believing yourself, you will begin to have confidence in your own choice, decision and action as you quest for greatness. For instance, when dealing with creative issues such as art, music, fashion and so on, your discerning mind will let you select the ones that best suit the occasion. In the same vein, your discerning mind can help you discern on great opportunities that may not be visibly open, for the public to grasp and utilized it. In an examination, when an apply question is posed to students, which demands the application of knowledge gain during a course of study, the power of discernment, may separate the extraordinary student from the average student.

On the contrary, if you are the type of person who does not have the believing power to discern on issues, almost all your decisions would be executed with the help of a third party, who may not be aware of the dreams and aspiration, you believe in. If you often rely on third parties for assistants, at times the suggested plan they have for you, may end in fiasco, unless all details of your ideas are fully disclosed to them, before informed decision suggested by a third party who has discerning mind, may work to perfection.

6. **It will help in identifying the root cause of issues**

Mostly, when an issue crop up, knowing the root cause is the first step in acquiring a long lasting solution to the problem. When you put your discerning mind to test, by analysing facts on the ground, it can clearly give you the power to identify the root cause of issues and urge you to devise solutions to these problems. That is why, believing yourself can assist you in your quest of finding the root cause of most problems, since due diligence will be done, with the help of discernment.

Therefore, taken the pains in making moves in identifying the root cause in every situation can be a trump card that may aid you to ascertain the truth in most situations. Once you identify the root cause, making an informed decision will not be difficult. Since, most decisions taken, after identifying the root cause, will mostly be the best.

7. **It can assist you to select and mingle with good friends**

The result of a discerning mind cannot be overlooked, since it comes with several benefits. This wisdom will guide you in your quest of finding good friends who will push you closer to your destination where most of the plans you have in life will come to pass. When you lack discerning mind, things will not augur well for you in life, unless you are smart enough to consult a discerning mind, before making important decisions in your life.

It takes just believe not in someone else but yourself, to step into the path that will lead you to the

land of discernment. This can only be possible if you can use your discerning mind carefully by selecting the right people who can influence you positively, as you toe the line of greatness.

Do you know that, at times, some people will come to you as friends with good intentions? Do you also know that, others will also interact with you as friends, with bad intentions? The wisdom of discernment will prompt you to subject them, under intense scrutiny and make good decision. Lacking a discerning mind, can spell doom for you, since the mistake you will make, may cause serious repercussion in your quest of achieving greatness.

Once you have seen the benefit of discernment, the onus is on you to do whatever it takes, within the realms of positivity to enable you reach your goals and aspirations. When you finally acquire a discerning mind, you will move from a myopic mindset, to a discerning mindset, when you apply discernment in your daily conversation.

Food For Thought

As you walk through life each day, dilemma will definitely come, when you least expect it. When the time is due for you to make a delicate decision that can have a significant impact on your life, I will entreat you to take a breather and use your discerning mind. When such time comes, a discerning mind may bring positive outcome. Therefore, the onus is on you to make that smart move during decision-making. Do you know that a decision made base on a discerning mind, often turn out to be the best? That is why believing yourself can give you the wisdom of discernment to equip you with confidence to make the right decision that will lead you into the limelight, where the greatness in you will begin.

On the other hand, someone who possesses a discerning mind, can assist you in one way or the other, to enable you make an informed decision. Hence, spending lots of time acquiring a discerning mind may be worth pursuing, since the advantages may far outweigh its disadvantages.

So take time and nurture your mind to acquire the tenets of discernment captured in this chapter to help you in your quest for greatness. If not for anything, your discerning mind can help you build trust with anyone you come across. Gradually you will be known as a trustworthy person.

Henceforth, most people will confide in you, by disclosing their personal problems for you to suggest a suitable remedy for them. Once you earned the trust of others, do not do anything that will betray your trust, but position yourself in a way that people can believe in you and trust your judgment.

"A Positive Mindset Will Always Navigate You Towards a Positive Lifestyle"
Richard Kyere-Boateng
Believing YOURSELF, the Beginning of GREATNESS

CHAPTER FIVE

Having a Positive Mindset

Life in totality, is about ones mindset, once you get your directions right, with the right frame of mind, it will guide you to make the right decision.

Therefore, feed your mind with the right words. Once you do, it will developed to a point that will bear positive fruits, which will serve as an obstacle to obstruct the activities of the negative minds. In life, it is not easy for someone to think positive in the midst of negative minds, but once you are determined to effect changes in your life, nothing can stop you, once you make up your mind.

When you begin the day on a positive note, it will give you the positive mood, needed to reach your goals and aspirations. That is why believing yourself is the starting point to all greatness, if only you will start your day with a positive mind. Therefore, if you believe yourself that you can make things work the way you want it to be, it will definitely work. That is why the scripture says, *"For as he thinks in his heart, so is he... (Proverbs 23:7)"* This simply means that, you are what you think. Henceforth, you can be the determiner that determines what flows through your mind, by attracting positivity in your day-to-day activities to enable you reach great heights in no time.

Do you know that, the things you think of each day, influence what you do each day? Do you also know that, what you do each day produces the results you will achieve

in that particular day? If you can allow positive thought to control your attitudes, actions and produce the ultimate results you are looking for, then you will reach great height sooner than expected.

Do you know that, Thomas Edison who created light bulb persisted and believed that he would succeed after failing several times? Edison had the positive mindset amidst the challenges he wanted to surmount. Throughout his innovations, he had a trump card, known as positive mindset, which gave him confidence and the power to succeed after failing on several occasions.

On the other hand, confidence can be nurtured by anyone who longs for greatness. For example if you start speaking confidently, sooner rather than later you will be a confident speaker.

You have to apply confidence in your daily conversation, by speaking and acting in a confident manner, if you are able to do this regardless of your audience, you will surely make an impact and boost your morale. When you do it frequently, your confidence will nourish your mind with positive vibes that will urge you on, as you journey through the storms of life.

Let us acquaint ourselves with how we can easily acquire a positive mindset. A positive mindset will always navigate you towards a positive lifestyle. After acquainting yourself with positivity, it will help you believe yourself even in the midst of challenges, where there seems to be no hope.

Once you inculcate the tenant of a positive mind, you will never throw up your hands in despair, but you will keep up the good work and soon, your positive lifestyle will direct your path to greatness.

1. Step out with confidence

You must always display confidence in every aspect of your endeavour. This will relax and free your mind from fear, failure and indecision. Confident persons, mostly have positive mindsets that allow them to believe in themselves. They are always ready to face life head on, without any hesitation. They often prepare ahead to meet opportunities as and when it surfaces.

The power that confidence bestows on us, as individuals, cannot be underestimated. As you learn to nurture positive mindset, it will gradually breed enough confidence to catapult you to greatness. Confidence will move the mental ideas captured in your mind to an action stage. During the action moments, your vision will then move swiftly from the mental pictures you dreamt of, to visible physical objects or products. When such time comes, people will be able to touch and feel it physically, with their senses. Once it is good and patronized by many people, it may finally shoot you to fame.

2. Look for positive aspect of every discussion

There is a saying that behind every problem there is a solution, this assertion is true and implies that, behind every negative statement there may be a positive one. So do not always look for negatives to judge someone but in every conversation, you must look for positive vibes which you can take home as a lesson for the day. To achieve an optimum performance during discussion, you can lean on your sense of touch,

smell, taste, sight and hearing. These senses can play a vital role in helping you to perceive with accuracy. For you to be able to sift through a discussion and come out with the positive aspects of it, you must engage all your senses when you find yourself in any discussion. When you put these senses to good use, it will often give you a clear picture of what you have perceived so far, when the discussion is over.

In the 21st century, in which we find ourselves, aside the natural sense that God has given us, technology has come in various ways that can also help in detecting senses that our bodies cannot experience. I will entreat you to use technology to your advantage, by inculcating them in your daily activities, when the need arises. Once you have these tools at your disposal, you will be able to perceive positive aspects of any interaction even, when they stretch beyond your reach.

3. Share positive messages with others

Do you know that practice makes perfect? If yes, why should you hesitate in sharing? Come on, step up your confidence and put into practice what you have learnt, by sharing it with others. As you share little by little, the message stays in your mind and become part of you. If you continue to share for a long time, it will become your habit and gradually, people will see and attest to it that, it is your true character trait.

Sharing will enhance both your intrapersonal and interpersonal relationship and create an avenue for a greater impact to manifest itself, once your message is worth sharing. Sooner rather than later, the positive vibes you are sharing may keep your enemies at bay and give you the freedom to explore all the positive ideas that will build your confidence and gravitate you towards greatness.

4. Relegate negativity to the background

Negativity is something that will never leave our community because as human beings we are not the same. One thing we must not forget is that, we also have different emotions and behaviours as we see, hear and experience life. Due to this, we are bond to encounter negativity in our daily interaction with people from every facets of life.

Do not be surprise to hear negative statement from people whom you thought will support you, because some of these debilitating statements are meant to pull you down and place you in a state of mental confusion. Therefore, it is relevant to relegate these negative words to the background, to allow positivity to take its rightful place. This positive attributes will then dictate the pace for your mind to follow and finally help you to soldier on, in times of challenges.

5. Live a positive lifestyle

We must live a positive lifestyle, a life that is filled with positive words and devoid of negativity. This in practical sense seems impossible. Living a positive life simply means, ignoring negative mindsets and embracing positive words that can have positive influence on your life. If you finally adopt a positive lifestyle, you will attract positive ideas, positive friends and finally make a positive impact. Once a positive impact has been made, due to your positive

lifestyle, greatness will surely be within your reach. The successful life you have always long for, will come to fruition. So do not compromise positive lifestyle for anything negative. If you are able to uphold this tenet, you will live a fulfilling life.

6. **Think differently**

Thinking differently will pave the way for you to do things in an extraordinary manner. Henceforth you may look, act and sound unique among your peers. In other words, it will give you the opportunity to look at things from a different perspective either than the norm.

As you face challenges each day, your actions and response to issues will be different from most of your peers because, you will always discuss issues with an opened-mind rather than a closed-mind. As a result, you will often anticipate not just one solution, but several options, before finally settling on the best.

7. **Let it go by stopping the blame game**

Blame game can never solve a problem. It always tells how low your thinking ability is, when challenges occurs. Therefore, instead of dissipating your energy on apportioning blame, you can channel that time judiciously in ways that can help you find solutions to problems that has come. This will help you save time and effort by focusing on ways of finding solutions to issues, than just apportioning blame.

Blaming others will always preoccupy your mind and draw you back, instead of moving forward to finding solution to a pressing issue, you will be there accusing others without making any conscious effort of working towards solving the problem.

Blame game will keep you as busy as a bee, when in reality you are busy for nothing, since that busy moments, may not result in anything profitable. In the end, you will never benefit from the blame game. You will only waste your precious time, which could have been channelled into a profit making activity that will yield good results in the near future.

8. **Spend time and reflect on your daily positive encounters**

At the end of a hard day's work, there is the need to take a sober reflection to reflect on the positive things that came your way during the course of the day. This will serve as a stimulus package that will rekindle your life and give you positive vibes to press on. Even in the midst of complete crisis, the positive things you encountered during the day, will calm you down and prepare your mind adequately for the next day. If you continue to do this, you will never fall prey to negativity.

When you take time to reflect on positive issues that came up during the day, you will cultivate the habit of a positive mind. These positive words, will serve as a silent motivational tool that will urged you to forge ahead in your daily pursuit. If you encounter any challenges, in your quest of achieving greatness, take a sober reflection of the positive words you met during the day, to help neutralize the situation.

9. Refined your inner critics

Everyone has an inner critic that always pushes him or her to look for faults in anything they come across, even when things seem good. This inner voice is mostly use by opinionated friends, as a great opportunity to unleash their negative words on you, which may send shivers down your spine and send you back to square one.

However, if you want to believe yourself in order to get the best out of any conversation, then you must fine-tune your mind in order to tame your inner critics. As you sift through the conversation in order to get the best out of it, you will benefit immensely, if you can tamed your inner critics.

Once you tame this inner voice, it will release you from the act of criticizing without bases, but when you learn to act positively, you will always discuss issues holistically, before using your inner critics, to give your final consent to the issues without prejudice.

The benefit of positive mindset, are enormous. Let us look at few of them.

a. Positive mindset breeds positive lifestyle

Once you have a positive mindset, it will influence you to live a positive lifestyle that is often devoid of negativity. When you tune your mind and focus on the positive aspects of life, your daily routine and interaction will follow suit and sooner than later, it will be part of you.

A positive mind breeds a positive attitude that finally results in a positive lifestyle. This will give you the power to speak positive words, positive affirmations and sing a song that contains positive lyrics. These positive attributes, when imbibe to the full, will help you in your quest for greatness.

b. It brings self believe

Positive minds often believe themselves in every step, decisions and choices they make. They think and act in a positive way. Above all, they attract positive things. It all boils down to the fact that, they believe themselves, as they journey gradually to greatness. The self-believe stimulate and shield them from any act by their adversaries to discourage them from pursuing their cherished dream. As a result of self believe, they tend to follow their lifetime dream willingly, without pandering to the whims and caprices of negative-minded persons.

c. It gives you the power to try again

When positive minds surrounds you, even when you fail, the positive attributes imbibe in you, will often urge you to try again. Aside that, positive minded people mostly have the notion that, anything they are working on will succeed, even when their adversaries think otherwise. In their quest to achieve greatness, if by any means they encounter failure, their positive minds give them the needed passion to try again. If you allow the power that positive mindset bestowed upon you to manifest itself in your life, it will strengthening you against any actions and inactions plan by your adversaries to ruin your life.

d. **It gives you the courage to forged ahead**

Positive minds are minds that are robust and often act in a courageous manner. They are not afraid to fail, so when opportunity comes their way, they master the necessary momentum and deal with the problem directly. This courageous nature, often urged them to follow their dreams and aspirations with all the zeal it deserved. Gradually, as they forge ahead, they may see their dreams come alive.

Do you know that, a positive mindset, can let it go, the various negative thought that have been harboured for years which is gradually sweeping every vestige of believe from you? If the response is yes, then make the necessary conscious efforts to keep these positive vibes, which may give you the courage to reach your goals.

On the contrary, if the response is no, then I will entreat you to imbibe them now, for in life, is better late than never to correct the flaws you have made in your life.

e. **It will distance you from negative lifestyle**

Positive minds, are always far from negativity, because they mostly restraint themselves from negative utterances. When they encounter negativity, their positive minds neutralized it.

The language of positive-minded persons is full of positive vibes, so when negative minds approach them with reasons why, their plans will not work, they disregard them and move on. They often dissociate themselves from debilitating comments that mostly emanates from the deceiving voices of the defeatist, which are mostly meant to ruin their dreams. They will never allow negative comments coming from their adversaries to take centre stage in their day-to-day activities, since they know the rippling effect of such comments.

f. **You will see things differently**

Your approach to issues will be different because positive mindset will nurture your nature to enable you perceive things differently. The way you analyse and comprehend issues will demonstrate the character of a positive thinker who sees potentials in the midst of trouble.

It all boils down to the fact that yourself believe, has taken you beyond the reach of negativity and has given you a new way of dealing with issues, by seeing things in a positive way. When others are seeing challenges within every problem, you will act differently because in most situations, you will see solutions within every challenge you come across.

All the benefits discussed above, will be waiting for you in due course, once you crave for positive mindset. The onus now rests on you to take up the mantle and forge ahead by embracing a positive lifestyle. This will propel you with the necessary energy needed to reach your goals and aspirations. If you allow positivity to be the driving force behind your dreams, you will soon attract positive ideas, exhibit positive gestures and gradually achieve positive results. This will finally give you a positive story to share to the world that will bring a major paradigm shift in the

minds of the teeming youth within your environs, who are losing hope in life.

We can do better as mentors, by demonstrating confidence using positive words, to enable us turn their motives into motivations that will finally give them the burning desires to soldier on in life. So, do not allow yourself to be manipulated by negative minds, as if you have no vision at all. For how long, will you continue to pander to the whims and caprices of these negative personalities, who are trying devious ways to draw you back, when you still have potentials, which are yet to be unlock? When you finally unlock these potentials, you will soon experience financial freedom and move on in life. From that moment, their negative words will have no place to occupy in your life, since your success story will keep them at bay.

Food For Thought

If positive mindset, become the attitude that drives your life, you will certainly attract positive results. That is why, you must be mindful of the things that drive your passion. In life, things that drive our lives, most often control our way of thinking.

For the most part of your daily activities, inculcate the lifestyle of the positive mind and you will begin to act, speak and react in a positive way that can trigger the greatness in you to begin. If you allow positive utterances to fill the empty spaces in your heart, you will only navigate towards good and positive results. When you allow positive mindset to preoccupy your mind, you will begin to display positive outcome. As a result, you will radiate self-confidence and be an optimist. From that moment onwards, greatness will be closer to you, than you ever imagine. You will not in any way share common attributes with the defeatist, who often harbour negativity, even when things are gradually getting better as days go by. So, do all you can, to inculcate these tenets, in your daily interactions, when you do, it will create a mindset that will be conducive enough to attract positivity.

If you heed to the advice emanating from this book and begin to imbibe the tenets of life captured within this chapter, by practising what you preach, these words of wisdom will nurture your nature and graduate you from being a pessimist to an optimist, where you will think and act in a positive way.

Believing
YOURSELF,
the Beginning of
GREATNESS

"...A Purposeful Lifestyle,
Will Always Define Your
Mission and Guide You
Towards Your Goal"
Richard Kyere-Boateng

CHAPTER SIX

Your Life Has a Purpose

Are you aware that, you do not exist for the sake of it? Well, if you are thinking otherwise, then I will entreat you to have a second thoughts because, there is a great purpose for your existence. When you realize that, your life has a purpose, it will then prompt you to know that, you are worthy of your existence and the world needs you badly, as you also need the world, in order to fulfil your goals and aspirations. If you value yourself and know that you were born for a purpose not a result of an accident, this can trigger the confidence you need, in order to believe yourself. Once you identify your purpose, do all you can to follow it, since a purposeful lifestyle will always define your mission and guide you towards your goal.

Next is to figure out, exactly what you want to achieve in life and then work towards it. After identifying your purpose, you can put it into writing to serve as a source of reference, when the need arises. Once your purpose is documented, it will then serve as a reminder that will prompt you to keep up the good work and gradually reach your goals and aspirations.

When you live a purpose driven life, any obstruction cannot stop you from pursuing your purpose because, you will not relent on your effort until you achieve the purpose you were destined to fulfil.

Below are some nagging questions that needs urgent solutions to enable individuals know the essence of their existence.

1. **Why are you here on earth?**

Why are you here on earth? Is a rhetorical question that is often asked by lots of people and the response is mostly relative. If you know your mission on earth as an individual, then you can battle life squarely with your purpose in mind. It sounds ambiguous, but if you take a cursory look at yourself, you will notice that, most of the features your maker gave you are unique and has been customize to suit your purpose. For instants, your voice, colour, height and facial features may often distinguish you from other people. That is not all, if we delved deep into your personality with regard to your interpersonal skills, you may be very different from others.

There are some hidden clues that can help you find your purpose, even when you still lag behind. You may be shy, sympathetic, generous, loyal, pragmatic, peacemaker and many more. These few words enumerated above, can help you discover your purpose. If the words describing your purpose are something to go by, then I can say without any doubt that, a clergy, a counsellor and a motivational speaker can be attributed to you as your purpose.

The way you react to an issue as and when it happens, may be different from how others may react to the same scenario. It will be a dent on your image, if you do not have any purpose to fulfil. That is why you need to identify your purpose and toe that purpose until a resounding victory comes your way.

2. What legacy do you want to leave?

Do you know that, some people sacrifice a whole lot of things, in order to leave a legacy and avoid the tendency of seeing their cherished dream goes down the drain?

If you ponder over the sort of legacy you want to leave, for generations to relish, it will always be a guiding principle that will regulate and direct your words, actions and emotions as you battle with life. It will often serve as a reminder, which will remind you of the positive impact that you want to make in life. This legacy will create the burning desires that will always urge you to believe yourself. You will now learn to soldier on in life when confronted with challenges.

Believing yourself will nurture you to know that, when the going gets tough, the tough get going, because you have a legacy in mind. As a result, you will press on until you finally achieve the bigger picture, set by you.

3. Are you content with your present condition?

Is good to be content with your state of affairs now, but if you are the type of person who wants to make a bigger influence and leave a great legacy, you will always crave for greatness. Once you reach the pinnacle of life, you will realize that, the impact you can make to people and the future generations are enormous. That is why, great personalities still long for

excellence to enable them position themselves strategically to reach out to many people who may need their support, to help them reach their set objective.

4. **Is there something else you can do to make the world a better place?**

    People who know their purpose in life know that, for their mission to see the light of day, they must work towards achieving it. The big dream they have in mind, often urges them to think of ways that will make the world in which they find themselves, be a better place to stay. This assertion urges them to be innovative by thinking outside the box whereas they revitalized themselves to fulfil their core purpose of which they were created. Since they have a burning desire to do something that will bring major changes in their community, country and the world as a whole, they then pursue their goals with a sense of urgency it deserved. This stimulates them to fulfil their purpose in life and make the world a better place.

5. **Do you believe in destiny?**

    If you have a destiny in mind to fulfil, then you must work towards achieving that destiny. If you are having the notion that, once your maker destined you to achieve a purpose, it will surely happen then you are joking. If you have an expected end ahead of you, this purpose will certainly drive you towards it, before it becomes reality. That is why you have a role to play in order to see your dream manifesting itself into life. For instance, if you are destined to collect money from a philanthropist, you can easily attest to the fact that, for you to get this money, you have a role to play. You can decide to go for it or not, the philanthropist will not force you to take that bold step. He/she will only give you an offer that will help alleviate you from the situation in which you find yourself, if you will oblige to his/her calling. The same can be said of what your maker has designed for you as the purpose for your existence.

The onus is on you to deal with the problem directly and cause things to happen in your life or decide to relax within your comfort zone and seeing your dream waste away in failure. In life, the final decision to reach your destiny by taking the right action rest on you. The same implies your purpose, once you know your purpose, working towards achieving this purpose, will take you to places.

At a specific point in our lives, we all have that bold step, which can change our lives forever, but what do we normally do, we approach opportunities with lackadaisical attitude and end up losing such chances. It all bores down to the fact that we do not believe ourselves. After pondering over these questions, it will help you figure out the purpose you were born to fulfil. In other words, you were born to fulfil a purpose, which also makes your existence meaningful.

Once you identify your purpose, you can now, lean on myriad of resources that your maker has instilled in you to leverage your activities as you toe the line of Greatness. All this plans can manifest itself if you look within you and begin to value what you have.

What you have often serves as your immediate resources. These resources can equip you to live a resourceful life that can help you work within the means at your disposal and still be effective and efficient, which will lead you to greatness.

Valuing what you have can lead you to your purpose

In life people don't value what they have, but value what they don't have. However, it takes what you have, to get what you don't have. Do you know that, you were born for a purpose? Have you discover your purpose? If you discover your purpose, you will realize that, God has given you the needed abilities, skills and interest. In addition, he has also position others in your life, who will augment your effort, to see you at the top.

Are you battling with life that is full of frustration, acrimony and hatred? I will entreat you to take a sip of water, relax and ponder over the issues at stake, to see whether you are in a wrong destination or not. If you finally find out that you are following the right purpose, then you only need to check your attitude toward others and make the right adjustment where necessary, to enable you stay focus until you achieve your purpose.

On the other hand, if you realized that you have toed the wrong career path, then take a quick detour and live a purpose driven life that will help you chance on the right purpose for your existence.

There are "do's" and "don'ts" you need to follow, if you want to value what you have. If you pay heed to these principles, you will know your value and become relevant as you focus on your purpose, to reach your goals in life without delay. First, let us look at the do's.

1. Be vigilant and open-minded in order to discover what you have

Do you know that, your friends can help you in your quest of identifying your purpose in life? That is why, you need to be vigilant and open-minded so that, when clues from friends, colleagues and acquaintances are coming from all angles you can easily identify them and take action as and when the need arises. When you stay focus in any discussion, your senses will be readily alert during conversations with friends, colleagues and acquaintances. Their comments can help you figure out what you have in terms of your skills, abilities and interests.

2. Your career should be carved around your abilities, skills and interests

If you want to find fulfilment in life and enjoy working moments during your life on earth, then it would be in your own interest to plan your career in such a way that, you will not be stranded each day, because of wrongful profession. If it happens like that, you will not be able to enjoy life to the full. In most cases, you will be battling with nagging problems such as stress, frustration and disappointment since your abilities, skills and interests may not be in line with it.

On the contrary, if your career is plan in accordance with your abilities, skills and interest, major problems that come your way, can easily be surmounted without any difficulties. In the end, your abilities, skills and interest will aid you to put up a stout defence against negative mind that may obstruct your efforts, as you quest for greatness.

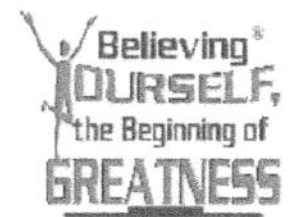

3. Be unique in your own way because your purpose is different from others

There is the need to be yourself as you stay original and follow the unique path that God has set for you. You need to learn, in order to appreciate who you are, as you battle with life. This can only come to reality, when you figure out that, your life has a purpose. In other words, you were born to fulfil a purpose that also makes your existence meaningful.

So go there with all the enthusiasm and prove to the world that, you have something valuable that makes you unique. This will urge you to believe in yourself and subsequently value what you have, which will gradually lead you to your destination sooner than you think.

4. Doing your purpose brings fulfilment

Have you discovered that, fulfilment brings inner joy, which may not be possible to buy with money? Do you also know that, doing your purpose may bring you joy and satisfactions?

Therefore, as you delved into life each day, you are likely to experience a relaxed mind that makes following your abilities, skills and interest worth pursuing. Through this, you will value what you have and come to realization that valuing what you have will always lead you to the things you don't have. After that, you will acknowledge the fact that, you were born for a purpose and valuing what you have will definitely lead you to discover your purpose.

After going through the "dos" that can help you in your quest for valuing what you have, I will urge you not to be oblivious to the facts enumerated above that makes your existence meaningful. When you follow these "dos" with all the zeal it deserves, the abilities, skills and interest you have that have not been utilized in all these years, will then serve as a catalyst that will lead you to your purpose. Once you identify your purpose with your skills in mind, it will be easy for you to toe that path to greatness. Without further ado, let us look at the "don'ts" to enable you avert obstacles that will drain your effort as you quest for greatness.

1. **Don't copy blindly because you want to be like someone else**

   At times, you look at what others are doing, and you follow suit. Is good to copy other good character traits and be like them, on the contrary, in a worst-case scenario, we copy blindly. If you copy blindly, which most people often do, you will end up choosing a plan, profession or destination that is not meant for you. Most often than not, people make these mistakes and find themselves in a profession which in reality, is not meant for them. In doing so, you will end up valuing what others have, instead of identifying your potentials. Therefore, don't just copy for copying sake, but copy someone, whose character traits and abilities, skills and interest are in line with your own.

2. **Don't imitate someone, until you discover your purpose in life**

   People imitate because they want to be like someone else. That person may have a vision, mission,

strategies and tactics, which you may not have any idea about it. Due to this, you may be imitating, but the basic components that will let you be like them, may be hidden from you. Besides, your vision, mission, strategies and tactics may be different.

After discovering your purpose in life, you can then imitate someone, whose purpose is similar to your own. Since you share similar purposes, imitating may not bring any major setbacks, because your vision, mission, strategies and tactics may be toeing the same line.

Don't imitate any bad character traits find in someone, but always look for the good character traits instilled in a person and follow suit. This will help you reach your goals and aspiration within a short period.

3. **Don't be in a field of work, where finding solutions to problems on daily basis always seem impossible**

When you find yourself in the right profession, where you are destined to be, problem solving mostly comes natural, with just a little effort. This happens because your career seems to match your inborn abilities, skills, and interest. These cardinal steps when utilized to the full, will finally bring fulfilment.

In other words, valuing what you have can help you perform effectively and efficiently as you follow your passion. That is why you don't need to push yourself in a field of work, where you are not destined to be. Once it happens like that, you will realized that, the ability for you to find solutions to problems on daily basis will always seem impossible because, your abilities, skills and interests are not in that area.

4. **Don't opt for what others have, but use what you have like your abilities, skills, and interests to reach your destination**

If you value the abilities, skills and interests you possess, you will achieve your purpose sooner rather than later.

On the contrary, if you pander to the whims of someone who is not moving in similar direction, you will be caught up in a career you never plan pursuing.

Half way into the job, you will realize that, you don't share similar abilities, skills and interest with the one you are following, as a result, you will later realize that, you have toed the wrong path. If nothing is done to avert the situation, you will end up at a wrong destination, which may not be your preferred choice.

This tells us that, if you opt for what others have, you will end up having things you don't need. Later in life, you will find yourself, at a place where you have never thought of going, but you have been misled by the abilities, skills and interest of others without giving it a second thought.

Therefore, wise up and value what you have and make critical decision with regard to your purpose based on your capabilities, to enable you reach your goals in no time.

5. **Don't value what you don't have, but value what you have**

Until you value what you have, it will be difficult to get what you don't have. What you have, form the basis, on which you can start something, that will

yield good results. By valuing what you have, it will energize you to believe yourself and have the notion that your life has a purpose. You then long for that purpose, which will lead you gradually to the destination you have set for yourself.

Once you finally achieve your purpose, the greatness that you have been longing for, in your lifetime will come to fruition. In the end, you will realize that, by valuing what you have and channelling what you have judiciously towards your purpose, it will draw you closer to greatness. Therefore, look within you and begin to identify the things you have, once you do, you will soon discover yourself and the real purpose for your existence.

6. **Don't draw conclusion on someone's destiny, if you don't know his/her purpose in life**

If you do not know the destiny or the purpose of someone, you tend to create a destiny for that person. At times, the plan you want an individual to follow, may not be the same plan that God has set for that person. That is why parents must always look at what their children have, for instance their abilities, skills and interests before choosing a career for them. If care is not taken as a parent, you will make a decision that may ruin your child's future. This is not only associated with children, because some adults follow love for money when it comes to career related issues with regard to their children's education.

Some parents mostly do not take into cognizance, the abilities, skills and interest of their children but instead, they allow themselves to be carried away due to their friends influence without carefully analysing the issue at stick, before drawing conclusion.

7. Don't underestimate your purpose

At times, majority of people when they identify their purpose in life, they tend to look down upon their suppose purpose. Bear in mind that, the purpose, of which your maker created you, is often meant to solve societal problem, in most cases. That is why, for the most part of your life, your purpose may sound, look and seems either bigger or smaller then you.

Never think of demeaning the purpose of which Almighty God gave you the abilities, skills and interest to fulfil your goals in life. If you by any means look down upon your purpose, you will be doing so at your own peril.

You may be the best option available at that specific moment, to drum home the purpose that will be of great essence to the society, the country and the world as a whole. Never demean yourself that your do not deserve that purpose, for all you know, you may be the chosen vessel suitable for the journey ahead of you, owing to the fact that, your maker, has already given you what it takes to surmount any challenges, as you quest for greatness.

When you take a cue from the various do's and don'ts listed above, you will come to terms that, you need to live a purpose driven life, in order to identified your purpose, in your quest of achieving greatness.

The purposeful lifestyle you have, will always navigate you towards your mission, if you will humble

yourself and pander to the whims and caprices of your maker.

Once you realized that your life has a purpose, you then live a lifestyle that will draw you closer to your purpose. After that, you must also implement this purpose with all the zeal you can think of, in order to reach your goal. Aside that, you must try as much as possible not to succumb to comments by those who do not know your purpose and the plans you have in mind. If at any point in time, if you bow to the pressures of negative-minded persons, their comments will be a setback that will lead you to failure.

At times, no matter how lengthy your explanation is, with regard to your purpose, plan or vision, they will not support you to carry on with it. In some instance, they will intentionally advice you to stop pursuing your ideas or purpose. If you oblige to their demands, you will never see major progress in your life. Others with genuine reasons will tactically enumerate several reasons why, it will not work. If it happens like that, take some time and do market analysis to see at first-hand, whether what they are saying is true or false.

Mostly, when you genuinely discover your purpose, it will be clear in your mind without any doubt, since it normally comes with a burning desire to implement it. Gradually, when this burning desire goes on and on, you will see the sign, become aware and respond to it. Sometimes, even when you are thinking of something else, your subconscious mind will draw your attention to it.

Life as we see is a cycle of influence, the life you are living will not be complete without touching the life of others. So live an influential lifestyle, by touching, inspiring and supporting others to help you discover your purpose.

Once you achieve your purpose, they will also achieve their own through your influential touch. When that time is due, the long awaiting legacy you want to leave will see the light of day. This act will actually send a message to your friends, relatives and the community in which you find yourself that you have really lived a purposeful life.

In the fullness of time, when myriad of ideas you have nurtured over the years begins to manifest itself, I will entreat you not to act in an egotistical manner by sending your ideas, skills and abilities that can impact positively on others' lives to the grave. Stand up to the test and make your presence felt, once you are alive and kicking. This will help you leave traces of influence, spearheaded by your purpose, for generations to relish when you are gone. From that moment onwards, beneficiaries will also take the mantle of life and cause things to happen. When such time comes, the influential journey you started some time ago will continue to live a life changing traces, as those you touched will also continue to touch others.

Do not forget that life is an influential journey that is why being influenced, in one way or the other can help your vision, mission and strategic plan see the light of day.

For all you know, we are all in a workshop of life that is training the trainers. Once the trainers acquire the skills and knowledge, they will then go out there and empower the weak to enable them realize their purpose by influencing them positively, with the knowledge acquired during the training. Therefore, do not break the chain of influence by acting selfishly, when you finally discover your purpose. Just step out with confidence and let your ideas reach others, in order to continue the cycle of influence, which will gradually reach greatness.

Food For Thought

In life, if you do not place premium on yourself, no one will value you. By seeing yourself as someone whom nature has endowed with a lot of skills, abilities and interest to face the challenges of life, your skills will serve as a tool that can help you discover the purposeful life you have been longing for, all these years.

Therefore, when the onus is on you to execute any good initiative accept it and do it to the best of your knowledge, in order to build good rapport within the community in which you find yourself. By so doing, you will gain recognition, respect and command a good reputation within your circles. When you live a purposeful life, you will be a living testimony for all and sundry to appreciate and mention your name as a role model to their children, when the time comes for them to pinpoint others who are living a purposeful life within their community.

You know in life, it does not cost anything to use what you have. I will entreat you not to be ignoramus and begin to act in an ignorant manner, when nature has instilled in everyone skills, abilities and interest.

You must master courage and delved deep into life and discover your purpose. As you do, you will move from a modicum of success to greatness. You will then be shock that all this while, you never knew that such a great talent is in you. If you discover your purpose and use the resources nature has given you judiciously, your maker will be proud of your astuteness and ingenuity.

Therefore, do not sit on the fence and react to things, as they unfold while you begin to display the lifestyle of the defeatist. Take up the challenge, discover your purpose on earth and begin to make a mark by causing things to happen as you fulfil your purpose in a splendid way.

Once you start causing things to happen, the myriad of challenges that surrounds your life will gradually fade away. This will finally make way for you to fulfil your purpose in life that will lead you to greatness.

So put away the fear that often give rise to failure and gather momentum with all the passion you can think of and work towards your purpose with a winning mindset, to enable you make a meaningful impact when your purpose is fulfilled.

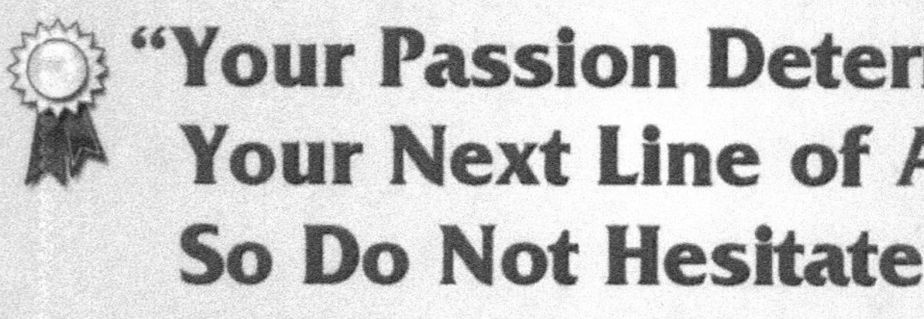

Ceremonial Swords

"Your Passion Determines Your Next Line of Action, So Do Not Hesitate to Follow Your Passion"
Richard Kyere-Boateng
Believing YOURSELF, the Beginning of GREATNESS

CHAPTER SEVEN

Follow Your Passion

After knowing that your life has a purpose, you can long for the purpose, which can easily be identified through your passion. In life, everyone is passionate about one thing or the other, but if you have the notion that, you do not have a passion then you must be kidding.

Following your passion to find a career is something that often brings contentment, which money cannot buy. You may be on the right track, if only the passion that drives your dream, is navigating you towards a worthy cause. That is why, if you are passionate about a job, that passion will urge you to believe yourself and then journey you towards greatness.

Passion is a strong zeal that energizes you to take initiative. This zeal, provides you with the needed believe that urges you to press on, even when it is time to close, you still love to continue. When you are passionate in the field you are working, you tend to love the job more than the payment that comes with it. Your dedication to duty, your quest for greatness and your relentless pursuance of perfection, are signs that you are following your passion. Your passion determines your next line of action, so do not hesitate to follow your passion. Therefore, let your passion dictate the kind of job you need to pursue until you reach the apex of your career.

Five important reasons why, you need to follow your passion, in your quest of achieving greatness, are listed below, follow it and you will soon see greatness in your life.

1. **It brings fulfilment, which lead to individuals believing themselves**

   Fulfilment comes when you follow your childhood dream that you have nurtured for years. You will soon be going places, if this burning desire is channelled in the right direction. When your burning desire, begins to move you towards a worthy cause, it will breed self-believe and self-confidence, which will gradually draw you closer to greatness.

   When such time comes, you will find solace in any task you undertake that are driven by passion. The passion you have will be the only motivator when confronted with challenges, while others think you have miss the mark. At that moment, your passion will be your companion. It will then act as a catalyst that will hasten your quest for greatness.

2. **Following your passion will help you surmount any obstacle that will come your way**

   Life itself is a problem solving activity, so if you are working in an area of endeavour, be aware that, obstacles are bound to happen. If the career, you find yourself in, is not the one you are passionate about, when an obstacle surfaces, in your line of duty, frustration will set in, if care is not taking, you will throw up your hands in despair. Since your interest is not there, nothing will push you to work with all the eagerness a passionate job will give you.

On the contrary, if challenges crop up in a field you are passionate about, you can easily whether the storm without any difficulties. All these may come to pass, when your natural abilities and your passion meets, they tend to create an emerging force that gives you fresh impetus, to move on in life.

3. Passion can let you work for long hours without you realizing it

If you are passionate about something, most often doing it comes natural. Because of the passion, the work now becomes a hobby and will always arouses your interest such that, you can work for long hours without you realizing it.

At times, when you are heading towards the closing moments of a task, even when it is late, your passion will still push you to long for extra period in order to complete a specific task. Your passion can serve as a good omen, which will help you finish any job ahead of schedule, thereby giving you an urge over your competitors who are not working in their passionate fields.

4. Following your passion can make your working life pleasurable

If you really want your working life to be exciting, stress free and satisfying, then you have to follow your passion. Do you know that, stress is something that is mostly difficult to cure, even with money? You can prevent stress in your working environment and other areas of endeavour, if only you will follow your passion in your quest of pursuing your career.

Your working life will be exciting when you follow your passion, since what you are passionate about will often bring excitement to you, once you pursue it with all the zeal it deserves.

If you are working in an area you are passionate about, there will be little or no stress at all, since ideas, motivations and hard work, will always follow you. Aside that, following your passion can also bring satisfaction to your body, mind and soul, as you soldier on in life.

As life goes on, your body, mind and soul will be following your passion, since you have interest in pursuing that career, you will not experience much pressure.

If you follow your passion, you will not often experience stressful life, as compare to others who ignored their passion during job search. Mostly, the love and interest you have for a particular job, will equip you to soldier on.

Even in times of financial difficulties, you will be relief of stress, because your passion will serve as a suitable substitute, which will comfort your body, mind, and soul. That is why Confucius said: *"choose a job you love, and you will never have to work a day in your life."* This assertion is true, because your working life will be like your leisure period. As a result, you will be less tensed and more relaxed in your line of duty, since you love doing it.

Therefore, let your passion lit your life and turn your hurdles into soothing moments, which will bring joy to you in your boring working vicinity.

5. Pursuing your passion enhance creativity and innovation

When your passion controls your words, actions and emotions as you long for greatness, new and original ideas will occupy your mind. You will then be spearheading a new dimension in your life.

From that period onwards, you will take great delight in creativity and innovation, as your imagination takes you beyond the norm to the extreme world. Your creative mind will then think outside the box, to help in identifying innovative ways of doing things. The creativity and innovative works, you are doing will soon be recognized by all and sundry as your creative abilities move you from being an ordinary creative person to a genius.

6. The fruit of your passion will linger on even when you are gone

Legacy is something that anyone can leave, but others don't just want to leave a legacy, for the sake of it. They really want to leave a legacy that resonates with all facet of life and continue to linger in the minds of the public when they are no more. In view of that, they stretch their imagination to the best of their abilities, which enable them to come out with something new. For example, people like Henry Ford, Aristotle, Shakespeare, Isaac Newton, Michelangelo, Leonardo de Vinci, Thomas Edison, Picasso and many more made the best use of their time, by following their passion.

Is your set time to pick up the pieces from several legends who made a name for themselves, their community and the world as a whole. Do not allow mediocrity to take over the creative and innovative skills your maker has given you, to die without making inroads into other people's life.

If you refuse to press on, with regard to the bigger dreams you have, it will be a dent on your reputation, if you die without a better legacy. If you really want to make a difference in this world, then the onus is on you to stand up and strive for excellence, by dint of hard work, the world will know you inside out.

Once you start making things happen in the best possible way, your voice will soon be heard from afar and the little effort you are channelling towards your passion will causes greatness to descend upon your life.

Food For Thought

Passion is the power that drives us to do something even when we are tired. As you follow your passion, major setbacks that confront you will soon give way to positive affirmations, great ideas and the power to press on without hesitation. That is why I recommend strongly that, you follow your passion by working in the field of interest. If you do, you will find fulfilment in your working life and the zeal to finish major project without much stress.

Your passion can help you sustain anything you wish to achieve and take you farther higher when greatness begins in your life. Therefore, never allow your passion to die of without implementing it to the later, once you do, the fuel that drives your imaginations to try something new while giving you the opportunity to discover yourself will come to an abrupt end. I will entreat you to channel your passion in the right direction and you will never regret doing it, since its benefits, far outweigh its disadvantages.

Once your passion is directed towards the right area or job, the tendency to fail, will be very low, as compare to others who do not follow their passion. So let your passion be in tandem with your goals and achieving it will be as easy as falling off a log.

Believing
YOURSELF,
the Beginning of
GREATNESS

"A Mentor Will Inculcate the Tenets of Life in You That Will Change Your Mindset and Give You a Professional Touch"
Richard Kyere-Boateng

CHAPTER EIGHT

Find a Mentor and Follow His/Her Path

After knowing your passion, it will be in your own interest to find a mentor, whose lifestyle is in line with your passion. If you comb through the world, you will realize that, no one can be a great person without the influence of others. That is why having a mentor in pursuance of your career, may give you greater advantage to acquire the experience, lifestyle and the remarkable courage of the mentor.

If you find your mentor, you can learn from him or her. You can then follow his or her path to greatness, by believing yourself. Although there may be slight hiccups here and there, if you endure these anomalies and stay focus without giving up your ultimate aims and aspirations, the greatness you have been longing for will come to pass.

When you meet the right mentor, he/she may be a great source of inspiration, information and personal coaching. If you ask your potential mentor for assistance, the tendency for him/her to accept and assist you, is very high, because they always have the view that, their efforts has been recognized.

Aside that, their contribution to their community, their area of study and the impact they have made in life has not been in vain. So do not hesitate to find a mentor, as and when the need arises.

A mentor can help in nurturing, directing and aid in the transfer of skills and experiences, to a mentee if a mentee can have a personal encounter with the mentor. Since mentoring mostly deal with personal and professional transformation, they can help you face challenges without much difficulty. A mentor will inculcate the tenets of life in you that will change your mindset and give you a professional touch.

Below are the qualities mentors bring on board, when their services are contracted.

1. **To assist the mentee to focus on the right direction**

   As a mentee, it will be prudent on your part to associate yourself with a mentor, who has seen it all in life. If not for anything, he can tune your mind to focus on your career and give you the needed directions to reach your destination in no time.

   You can also achieve the same objective, without a mentor, by applying the trial and error techniques. If you opt for the trial and error method, you are likely to spend several years, wandering around in search of the right career path until you finally find an antidote, to your predicament. That is why finding a mentor is crucial, in your quest of achieving greatness. Once you chance on a mentor, he/she will guide and direct your effort in a proper direction as you quest for greatness. For all you know, you may be channelling your effort in the wrong direction. That is why a mentor's role in your life, can cause major positive changes in your career development. A mentor will guide you on what you must do to stay focus, and finally acquire the needed experience and expertise.

It is essential for mentee to find a mentor, who will guide him or her to focus on the right direction, as he/she quest to achieve greatness in life. The nurturing you will receive from a mentor may help you to achieve the best in your chosen career within a short period. So stop bragging, and humble yourself under the tutelage of a mentor, to enable you reach your goals and aspirations in shortest possible time.

2. **To give credit where credit is due**

A mentor is supposed to guide and give advice, as and when the need arises. Therefore, if during the tutelage he/she realized that there has been improvement in your nurturing, he/she will give you the needed encouragement and praises in order to urge you on. This can help you keep track of the progress that you have made so far and what lies ahead of you in real time.

A mentor will certainly praised you, when you deserve praises. A word of caution to the mentee when you begin to receive praises, admiration and encouragement from your mentor, do not be swollen-headed and have the notion that you know better than the mentor has, but learn to be humble and submissive to your mentor to enable you achieve your goals and aspirations in no time.

3. **To criticize constructively in the quest of nurturing the mentee**

When a mentor realized that you are moving at a slow pace or your efforts is below standard, he/she has the power to urge you to work extra hard in order to meet

the standard. This constructive criticism is not intend to kill your spirit, but is meant to correct the flaws in your efforts in order to put you on a sound footing.

Therefore, during mentoring, be prepared to accept constructive criticism that can shape your mind, emotions and attitudes. When you meet your mentor, you should be mindful, be sober and observant, under his/her tutelage. As you go through the studies in a careful manner. These character traits may instil in you, the learnable spirit that will give you the morale to acquire the skills, expertise and ethics needed to soldier on in life and become a victor.

At this stage, the mentor will then probe into the affairs of the mentee, in order to know at first-hand, the relevant previous knowledge, that the mentee is bringing on board, to enable him/her clarify, advise and guide him/her to make an inform decision. These constructive criticisms, when they are accepted in good faith by the mentee, may help him or her acquire the virtues of life that will serve as a guide later in their professional life. The virtues acquired will clear your mind from complacency and set a high standard for you to follow as you quest for greatness.

4. **To instil discipline and high values in you**

A mentor will inculcate high moral values in you that will discipline you to abide by the principles of the job. This can be achieved, when a mentor sees the mentee as a friend.

In order not to fall short in your personal development as a mentee, one only needs to acquaint him/herself with the rules and regulations that govern both your personal development and professional practice. This will make you a man of principle and become familiar with the ethics of your practice.

These higher values may come handy later in life that will enable you to uphold the tenets of your career. Once you do, it will equip you to speak, act and execute all your services in an astute way. This little touch, by the mentor, can bring a change of mindset that will let you toe the professional way of doing things, which most people lack.

5. To spend quality time with the mentee

A mentor must have much contact hours with the mentee, in order to have a positive influence on the mentee. This can easily be achieve, if the mentor takes the mentee as a friend. Through friendship, the mentee will be able to relate easily with the mentor to achieve a common objective.

When the mentor and the mentee build a symbiotic relationship from the onset, various attitudes and skills will be uncovered. As these traits manifest itself, the mentor will then prepare a suitable remedy, to fix any anomaly that can later be a setback in the professional life of the mentee, as the tutelage goes on. This quality time may go a long way to instil the prerequisite skills needed to make the mentee, a holistic person. Therefore, when the opportunity comes for you to connect with a mentor and learn the tenets of life, do not hesitate to do so, just embrace it with all the urgency it deserves and your life will never be the same.

6. To recommend the mentee

A mentor's recommendation after days, months and years of nurturing can open doors for you. As a mentee, you need to build a good rapport with your mentor, so that even after the nurturing, if any opportunity comes in his/her line of duty, your name can ring a bell in his/her mind for him/her to recommend you for a greater pursuit.

Do not be oblivious to the fact that, your mentor has seen it all in life and has already build a network of influential professionals, at times across the globe. Since they are known in real life as movers and shakers, if you get the opportunity to work with them, it may draw you closer to greatness.

Many professionals were employed through the recommendations of their mentor, under whose networking, pave the way for outstanding mentee's to occupied positions they never thought of acquiring. Therefore live a courteous life, that is worthy of recommendation, to capture the attention of your mentor and gain recognition, when the need arises.

As a mentee, there are certain things you need to know when the opportunity comes for you to undergo training under a mentor. Study them to acquire the skills and experiences that will guide you to greatness.

1. As a mentee, your relationship with your mentor must be reciprocal

In communication, when a sender sends message the receiver receives the message he/she then send a feedback to the sender for communication to take place. In reality, the mentee upon receiving the message must send a reply to the mentor for the conversation to flow.

Therefore, as a mentee, you must always stay glue to the conversation as and when, the need arises. Once the message reaches your end, you then respond adequately to the question, while you keep in touch with your mentor throughout the conversation, with a follow up question. When a follow-up question, comes after several minutes of listening, it creates the impression that you have interest in the discussion, as your mentor walks you through the tutelage.

2. **As a mentee, listen, observe and jot down some essential points**

You must listen with rap attention, observe every little detail and write down points that are of paramount importance to you. After writing down these salient points, you can refer to them later on, in times of need. When you continue to jot down these points frequently, your mentor will realize how serious and dedicated you are towards his/her tutelage. This will further urged him/her to give in his/her best, since your mentor would be certain that, the efforts that has been put in place, would surely yield good results.

3. **As a mentee, you must be punctual at all your meetings with your mentor**

Punctuality creates the impression that, you are totally committed in acquiring the requisite knowledge, which will help in your journey to

greatness. Aside that, punctuality may speak volumes about you to your mentor, because it will pre inform him/her that, your word is your bond. In this regard, he/she can recommend you to a company, since you have made a distinct mark that makes you a valuable asset to any company that may chance on you.

If you stay reliable, capable and punctual about your service delivery or work out put, your mentor can recommend you at any point in time to a company or influential personalities, who may change your status quo.

4. **As a mentee, you must be ready to psych your mind up for criticism**

Criticisms are inevitable, when it comes to nurturing and training of an individual or group of people. As a learner, you are bound to make mistakes. That is why when such thing occurs, the mentor must place you back on a sound footing, with constructive criticisms.

In fact, the prime objective, of constructive criticism is to correct the flaws in your life and allow you to grow from strength to strength which may finally help you to reach your destination.

The challenges of life seen each day can easily be surmounted with little effort, if you can tune your mind, in a more astute way. Mostly, great people have the notion that everything in life stem from the mind. So in your journey to greatness, if during your interaction with your mentor you go through criticism, do not let your heart be troubled, since in most case, these criticism are meant to fortify and prepare you for the task ahead in your career.

5. As a mentee, you must be able to share your benefit

After acquiring all the necessary tutelage from a mentor and have secured a job, it is now time to share the knowledge you have accrued from the services of your mentor to others who may need your service in one way or the other. This is crucial, since sharing is caring, as you share, the more knowledgeable, you become, if you continue to share, it will boost yourself confidence and draw you closer to greatness.

Let us not be blissfully ignorant about the fact that, we are all a testimony of influence. In life, no one can leave without the support of others. There is no one on this earth, who has not been influenced one way or the other by a teacher, a pastor, a sheikh, classmate, friend, mother, father, uncle, brother, sister, husband or wife. So once, you rise through the system to become a mentor, the onus rest on you to pass the chain of influence towards others, to help in their nurturing toward their journey to greatness.

After knowing the role of a mentor and a mentee, you will all bear with me that, if the symbiotic relationship that exists between them is well grounded in friendship, it will benefit the mentee during the time of nurturing. The chain of influence that a mentor passes on to the mentee, will give the mentee the determination he/she needs to enable him/her, reach new heights. Adhering to this golden rule can help the mentee put into practice the experiences acquired from the mentor and finally save the mentee from several years of struggling.

Life without a mentor is full of stress, naivety and mediocrity. You may pass through a stressful life, but it

would be difficult to de-stress, without the directions of a mentor. At times, your naivety will crop up when a challenge beyond your skills and understanding manifest itself. Your inexperience will expose your flaws at the workplace, when you reject the tutelage of a mentor. Therefore, do all you can to acquire the services of a mentor. Once you do, you will soon reach your goals and aspiration.

Food for Thought

If you finally find a mentor, he/she will save you days, months and years of stressful life, which normally comes due to your inexperience nature as a mentee. When you humble yourself under his/her tutelage you can, easily fix most of the mistakes that took your mentor several years in fixing during his/her youthful days as an amateur.

With many years of working, training and the experiences gain over the years as a mentor may be revealed to you, once you pander to his/her whims. Through dedication and submissiveness, several tips, tricks and techniques that can aid you in surmounting various challenges, will be disclosed to you, if only you will humble yourself under your mentor's tutelage.

Arrogant mentees, mostly loose the opportunity of tapping into the experiences of their respective mentors. If something baffles your mind during the tutelage, be bold and find out. Always ask relevant questions that are related to current issues under discussion. If the right questions are asked at the right moment, it will trigger the right response that will help you stay within the scope of the conversation and be accorded a relevant response. If you have a question from previous lessons know the appropriate time to ask.

Therefore, I will entreat you to study the mood, the body reactions and the environment, before posing a question for your mentor to respond. If there is a cordial relationship between a mentor and a mentee, then proper tutelage may transpire without much difficulty.

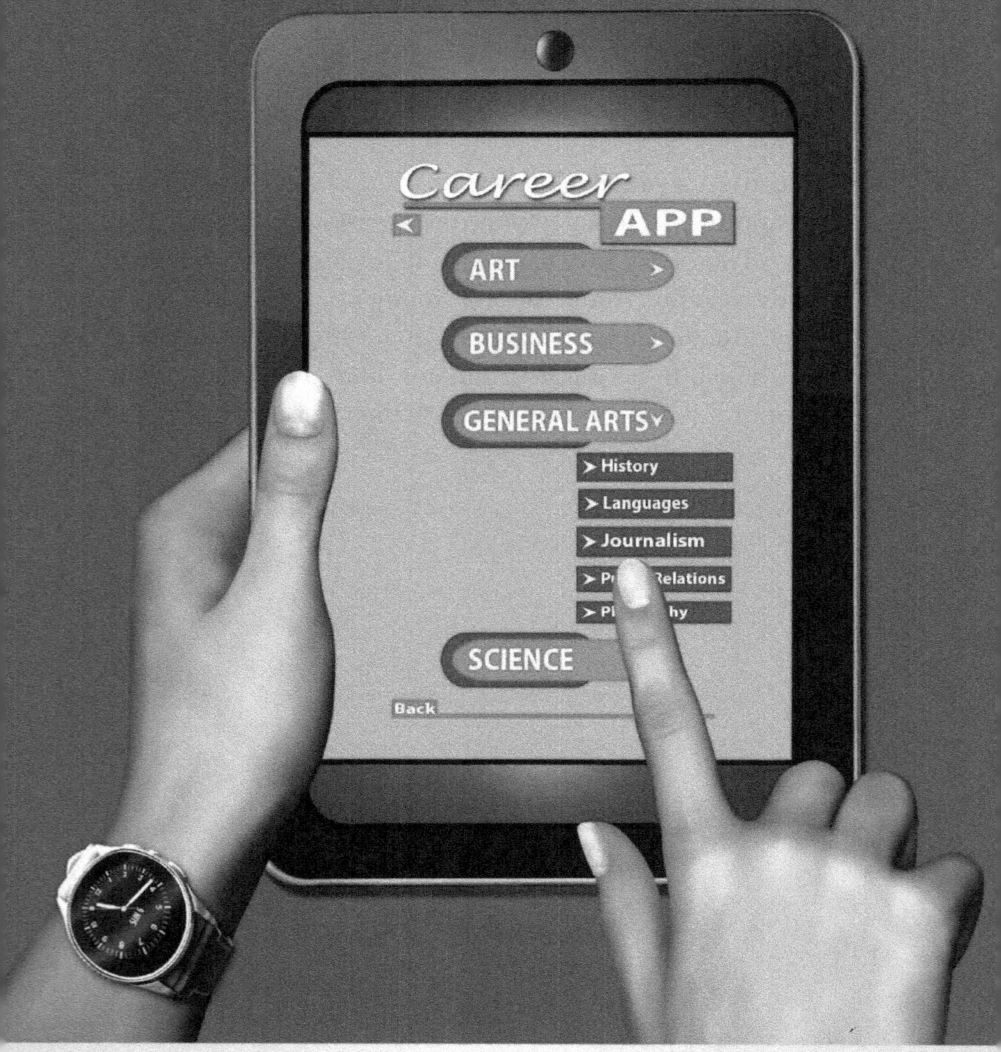

"Identifying a Suitable Career that Takes Cognizance of Your Skills, Abilities and Interest, Can Bring Fulfilment"

Richard Kyere-Boateng

CHAPTER NINE

Finding a Career Path

Choosing a career is a daunting task but when plan carefully can lead to a brighter and prosperous future. After finding your mentor, you will know the exact career to pursue and follow it.

In the 21st century, in which we find ourselves now people no more, spend all their lifetime working for one organization, most often professionals change their job titles throughout their career life by working for different industries or institutions. Some are due to the fact that, they are not comfortable with their old work schedules, others also change their job titles due to a new burning desires they have find elsewhere.

At times, your academic progression, can lead to a change in job title, as one progress academically, their job titles changes to much their new reputation. In most cases, change happens when someone make quick progression in his/her academic life.

It all boils down to the fact that, human beings have many desires and are trying day in and day out to fulfilled them. Identifying a suitable career that takes cognizance of your skills, abilities and interest, can bring fulfilment. Before you follow, the steps below to enable you select your career path, first ponder over these questions and let it be at the back of your mind as you launch a search to find your career.

1. **What are you good at and love doing most?**

If you know yourself better than anyone else does, then you must be able to answer this without any hesitation. For example, are you good in communication, interpersonal skills, managerial skills, science, mathematics, designing, then ask yourself whether you have passion and love for it? If yes, just narrow it to a specific career. For example, if you are good in managerial skills, then you can channel all your effort towards becoming a managing director of a company.

On the other hand, if you realize that, you are good at communication, you can then focus your attention on becoming a public relation officer, an author, journalist, and so on. In life is also good and interesting when you choose a career in your area of interest. This will make your working vicinity be an area where creativity dwells. If you are able to carry on with these basic principles, the environment in which you find yourself, within your working life, will be a place where you will soon experience the smiles and the bliss you have been missing all these years.

When you notice this at an early stage of your life and decide to choose your career base on the things you are very good at doing and love doing it often, toeing this path as a career may be the best option.

2. **Which working environment best suit your persona**

You have to link your character traits to a career you wish to pursue. For example if you are jovial in character, you will realized that, career that will let you interact with others will be a perfect one that will suit your career path. We all know that jovial people easily relate to people as they come across them, so interacting with others may be a job that can put smiles on your face.

The environment you want to work in life can draw your attention to the career you wish to pursue. This can give you a gist on the career that best suit your personality. You then delve into it, to know the details of this career whether it would be worth pursuing, when you find yourself in this working environment. For instance, if you always love to explain and discuss issues with people, then journalism, teaching and public relations can be a working environment that best suit your persona.

On the other hand, if you love adding, subtracting and dividing numerical values, then statistics, banking and finance can be a working environment that best suit your persona.

In addition, if you are creative, witty and innovative, the best working environment that can easily connect with your persona includes art, science, journalism, music and the film industry.

You must find out the working environment that best resonates with you and carve your career around it. If you do, you will find fulfilment in your working life. When you opt for a career that primarily takes into consideration, the working environment that resonates with your personality, fulfilment will come natural. Those who choose their career, without taking into account, the working environment that

best suit their persona, often find themselves wanting. Others get to know this, after few days of working in a stressful environment. So wise up, take your cue from this and make the right decision that will lead you to the right career path.

3. Can your lifestyle fit the career in perspective?

You must always ask yourself this question, before choosing a career. This will give you a prerequisite information that can help you make the right choice.

Bear in mind that, the way you live your life in relation to your character, habit and your physical outlook can serve as a guide, which will assist you to toe a career path that takes into account your actual lifestyle. For example, if you are tall, slim, pretty as picture and have great command over the English language and other languages, modelling, acting, news anchor can be a perfect match.

This charming personality of yours and the fluency you have in language, all coupled with yourself confidence can help you excel in these types of careers. If your lifestyle is not taken into consideration, and you pursue any career, your working life, will not be pleasurable.

4. Where you want to settle in life

The exact location or environment where you want to live with your family, can affect the type of career, you may pursue. For example, if you dream of living a simple life in a countryside, which is devoid of city life, then it would be difficult to choose a career that is mostly found in the cities. If your place of abode is the countryside, then careers like public relations officer, modelling must not be careers to consider.

On the contrary, if you love to enjoy city life to the full, then public relations officer, modelling and others can be the best option. Your anticipated place of abode, can in one way or the either, have effect on the type of career path you will toe.

5. **List all the possible careers on your mind**

When you yearn for the career you love to pursuit, listing and eliminating can be a method that can easily assist you in your quest of following your career path. You can list all the careers on your mind and eliminate the ones you do not want to pursuit.

After eliminating those that do not have direct bearing on the career you are longing for, you may finally have a visual representation of the career you wish to pursue. You then continue the elimination until you finally settle on the right career.

Clues to look for, when choosing a career

When the time comes for you to select a career, the selection process must be done, with your abilities, skills, and interest in mind. In most cases, the career you have in mind may be the right career you love to pursue but for all you know, the ones you do not want may be surrounding it.

Therefore, I will entreat you to select the best among the rest. Aside that, the environment you wish to work, the number of years it will take for you to acquire the skills needed to qualify you as a professional in this field, need to be carefully analysed.

When you ponder over these clues, your final selection will be the one that best resonates with you. Check out the clues explained below.

1. **Follow what excites, boosts and whip your interest**

In life, what really arouses your interest can be a perfect much for your career. You will end up loving what you do and at the end, greatness will be your portion. If you do a reality checks on great personalities, it may interest you to know that, majority of them, followed a career that had direct relations with their interest. Most of them became great after deciding on positive things that whip up their interest.

Are you stacked in the stressful job you are doing now? You can make amends to the predicament you are experiencing now, by following your interest. Bill Gates of Microsoft and Steve Jobs of Apple drop out of school just to follow things that excites and whip up their interest. Henry Ford also broke away as an employee from the company he was working with and then followed his interest. Finally, he created a successful company known as Ford.

If you follow the bandwagon, there is no way that you can stand out from the crowd if you really want to be noticed, because the crowd you are itching to lead may now be leading you.

Briefly, you will just be selling your leadership right to a group that does not seem to be making any headway. If things continue to fall apart, your cherished dreams and aspirations will disappear into the thin air, without you realizing it.

2. Follow your abilities and skills

What you are good at, can give you clues on which career path to follow. When you follow the gift you possess and things you value with your passion in mind, identifying your career will not be a huge task. Once you have these at the back of your mind, your instincts will capture it and help navigate you towards that path. Therefore, I will urge you to follow your abilities and skills to enable you identify your goals.

As you long for greatness with your believe in mind, be vigilant to enable you recognize your capabilities as you search for the right career. Once your career takes cognizance of your skills and abilities choosing a career based on these attributes may help you toe the right career path that will lead you to greatness.

3. Make a career plan

You can make a career plan that has time lines, needed to walk you through the skill acquisition period. This referred to the number of years required, for individuals to acquire the skills, to enable them practice these profession, which will help them achieve their goals or purpose. This may give them, a general overview of the career they wish to pursuit, within the period, things they will need, in order to reach their goals and aspirations.

In short, what the plan seeks to do is to pre-inform you whether you can dedicate the time or period needed to acquire the training that will lead you towards the set career. For instance, if you want

to become a Lawyer, a Nurse, a Medical Doctor and so on, the time line for schooling or skills acquisition may definitely vary. The onus is on you to choose the one that is dear to your heart, to help you execute the plan without delay.

4. **Interview a professional**

You can interview a professional, who has excel in your field of interest or is a master of the career of your interest. For example a bank manager, a teacher, an artist, a medical doctor, a graphic designer, a chartered accountant, a musician and many others. Since they have pass through the system before, they can save you years of frustration.

A professional's narrative may touch on the good and turbulent moments he/she has experience in life. If you are able to learn from the mistakes committed and the successes chalked by the professional so far in life, by adopting the pros and avoiding the cons, it will equip you to face life head-on. The experience you will tap form him/her, may let you know the courses to select, at the basic and senior high school level, institutions to attend at the tertiary level and programmes to offer, in your quest of pursuing your career path. If not for anything, at least they can guide you, to avoid their mistakes.

A mentor may give you the tips and tricks that have been gathered over the years, through good and turbulent moments in his/her career life to help you succeed in life.

5. Take a career test

When you take a career test, it will pre-inform you on the areas you can easily excel. The test will walk you through series of steps, which will guide you to answer questions ranging from leadership, managerial, language, communication, arithmetic, interpersonal, intrapersonal, creativity, innovation, science and technology.

After answering these thematic questions in these areas of your life, the result will help you in your quest of selecting the career that best suit you, based on the response. This result, can point you to a career you love but not currently available on your mind.

This test can be down online, for instance, you can search for series of career test site using search engines like Google, Yahoo, Bing and many other search engines that will help you locate these test resources that may guide you to make an informed decision.

You can also search directly if you have the site address of the test institution such as http://www.careerfitter.com, career apps on Google Play Store and Apple Store, which at times comes with a small fee when an individual sign up to take the test. If you discuss a career test with a mentor, he can take you through the process for you to take the test. There are some tertiary institutions where career test can be taken.

On the other hand, don't go round in circles when you are confronted with career issues. Remember that, career experts and consultants may be readily

available to assist you, when you get in touch with them. They will give you all the solution you may need to make an informed decision, when the need arises.

Therefore, when you get the opportunity to do the test, do not hesitate, just do it and sooner rather than later, you will be able to identify the true career, you are longing to pursue.

6. Go on internship

You can go on attachment to a company or institution that is providing a service that relates to the career you want to pursuit. Take note that before, during and after the internship, it will pre-inform you whether you can survive, if your abilities, skills and interest take you there. This will give you, hands on experience to know whether you are on the right career path or not.

Most often internship gives students a holistic approach to the career they wish to pursuit. During this period, they normally work with experts, in various departments. These experts offer themselves as mentors by assisting the student, to open up themselves to questions and receive feedback where necessary.

Aside that internship gives students the opportunity to experience the world of work during their course of study. It also help student to make an informed decision, about the career they want to pursuit.

At college, when a window of opportunity comes for you to go on internship, treat it with all the needed urgency it deserves. That is the time you can try your hands on a daily routine or task perform everyday by the company.

All the points explained above, are potentially viable to help you in your quest for the right career path. As you long each day in search of the right career, I will urge you to open your mind to all possibilities that will lead you to the best career. Mostly, when it comes to choosing a career that resonates with you in totality, ideas relating to your career path can be tapped from friends, acquaintances, family members, the religious societies you belong to and the community in which you find yourself. Others include classmates, teachers, mentors and many more. Their utterances can help you discover your career path without much stress.

On the contrary, if you are a close-minded person, even when all indications, from people of diverse backgrounds, are pointing your abilities towards a certain career that best fit your way of life, you will ignore them completely, without giving it the considerations it deserves. For all you know, you may be taken a primrose path, which may not augur well for you in the near future. In the long run, your closed-minded attitude may block the good suggestions that may help you find your career path.

If you listen to the various clues coming from them, without any prejudice and giving it the benefit of doubt, you can take a cue from their recommendations to help analyse their concerns to the best of your knowledge. At times, their advice may save you years of regrets, agonies, and depressions. In some weird situation, their directions can spell doom for you. Whatever the case may be, you have to

discern on them and draw the needed conclusions to help find the right career path.

A sober reflection of your life, will give you a vivid account of who you are, where you want to be in life and the kind of job you can easily do. You must ponder over these things thoroughly, before choosing the right career path when the need arises. When you pursue the right career, with all the zeal it deserves, your purpose in life will be accomplished in no time.

Do you know that, career that resonates with your skills, abilities and interests, will make your life comfortable? Therefore, choosing a career may require an ample time, a well thought of strategies and a discerning mindset, which will help you sift through issues and select the best option. Once you get your career right, all other benefits will follow in due course. This will calm your nerves and create an enabling environment, which will breed a successful career life that will take you to greatness.

Food For Thought

If you finally identify the right career, your journey to greatness will be closer than you ever thought. Hence, I will entreat you to research into the career you are passionate about and check whether the environment and working conditions can suit your persona. Most of the nagging questions that relates to the career you wish to pursue, can be ask during the training with the mentor.

When your career also take cognizance of your skills, abilities and interest, finding the right career, will not be as difficult as your anticipation may put it. Your abilities, skills and interest can do all the tricks that will help you in your quest of identifying your career path. That is why being open-minded, can help you notice the little clues that may come from others, who have been closely monitoring you.

On the other hand, if you are close-minded, you may often miss genuine clues that may come from this crop of friends you have within your circles. For all you know, the comments and response from friends, co-workers, and family members, may give you clues with regard to the career that best resonates with your lifestyle.

If you find yourself in a dilemma with regard to the career path, you love to toe then, I will urge you to take a cursory look within yourself and select the one that best suit your persona. This can easily be identify based on your instinct while you tread cautiously, once your inner voice prompts you to do so. When things becomes tough in life as a novice, in regard to your career path, an interview with a professional will bring a huge impact in your life as you launch a search for the right career path.

Do you know that, at times, life can be full of frustration, if you choose the wrong career path? That is why matters that have to do with your career, needs a deep thinking and a concerted effort to enable you follow the right career path, which will lead you to greatness.

"...Be Different to Make a Difference in Others' Lives That Will Linger on, From Generation to Generation"

Richard Kyere-Boateng

Believing YOURSELF, the Beginning of GREATNESS

CHAPTER TEN

Daring to be Extraordinary

In life, being extra ordinary cut across all areas of human life, from childhood, adolescents and adulthood. Extra ordinary is also seen in areas like education, creativity, science, entrepreneurship and other facet of life.

If we dare to be extra ordinary, it will lead us to greatness, because great people have the extraordinary character traits that help them to succeed in most of the things they set out to do. When you delved into the life of extraordinary people, it will be prudent to touch briefly on four facet of human life, where being extraordinary can help you reach any goals you venture upon. These areas include the life of an entrepreneur, a creative person, a parent and a student. If you dare to be extra ordinary in these thematic areas any impediments that come your way, in your quest of pursuing greatness may be cleared in no time.

Once these impediments are behind you, your daring lifestyle will lead you to greatness. So, be different to make a difference in others' lives that may linger on, from generation to generation. The difference you will make will spark an attitudinal change in the life of the people in the community and beyond.

As an entrepreneur

A dream nurtured by an entrepreneur can often happen, if they believe in themselves. The entrepreneur must put his

or her statement into achievable goals, by venturing into a risk. When you believe in yourself as an entrepreneur, there would be a sense of urgency that will inspire, rejuvenate and increase your energy to press on until you reach your goals.

Do you know that, an entrepreneur is someone who looks for opportunities by carefully analysing the environment, seeing what is lacking within his/her surroundings and making an effort by undertaken a risk, in providing what is lacking, to create profit? All the analyses done by an entrepreneur will never happened until the entrepreneur takes bold steps towards greatness, by hitting the ground running and not just talking for the sake of it, but implementing ideas he/she has raised.

As a creative person or inventor

Creativity or invention deals with how passionate, curious and adventurous you are. For creativity to take place, one needs to belief him/herself in order to have outside the box thinking. Believing yourself can help you dare to be different while given you a slide urge over your competitors. If you dare to be extra ordinary, by adding extra touches to your creative imaginations when starting a project, you will soon be a great genius of your time. The creative works or inventions you have done, may take you to places you least expect to be. Therefore, make good use of your creative and inventive skills and sooner than later, it will catapult you to successes you have never dreamt of achieving.

As a parent

You must dare to be different in order to be a mentor to your family and the entire neighbourhood. It may take extra effort to enable you acquire a competitive urge over your competitors or acquaintances. Through this, your family will believe in you. This will inspire you to go the extra mile to be a great asset to them.

If you dare to be extraordinary, your children who are schooling will try as much as possible to emulate your gestures and become a better person in the near future. This will make the nurturing of both your children and those in your neighbourhood easier, because they will look up to you as a father, role model and a mentor, due to the exemplarily life you have shown within your neighbourhood.

As a student

Being extraordinary as a student, can take you to places you never dreamt of going. That is why every student must have the daring spirit that will inspire him or her to thrive for excellence, in the midst of challenges. After knowing the impact that being extra ordinary in your field of work can bring, we can now turn our attention to twenty-one (21) qualities of an extra ordinary student. This is to help save, the dwindling fortunes of education in Ghana, Africa and the world as a whole.

Have you ever question the status quo why, students sit in one classroom, with one teacher, one syllabus, one question and one examination. Nonetheless, at the end of the exams, when the results come out, there are always varied outcome. Student who get grade "A" continue to get "A" whereas those who get grade "F" continue to get "F". That is why, if you continue to do the same thing every day, you will continue to get the same results. This assertion seems weird but that is the absolute truth.

If the plan or strategy that you are using in your academic pursuit, is not bringing you the right results, change and embrace the qualities of an extraordinary student. For the extraordinary, they know that, every great achievement comes from the mind due to this, they are mindful of their choice, attitude, and above all, they are disciplined.

For the most part of our academic pursuit, majority of students cherished the lifestyle of the extraordinary student, as they give them all sort of names ranging from genius, intelligent, assertive and talented. One funny aspect of it is that, in Sub Saharan Africa, the extraordinary students are mostly referred to as witches and wizards. They are of the view that, extraordinary students are naturally born with a supernatural power to excel in their academic pursuit. To some extend I bet to differ because, there are basic principles that, the extraordinary student follow in order to be different and outstanding among their peers. Some of these principles are inborn whereas others acquired their skills through learning, in order to be extraordinary.

Our lesson stem from the fact that, we can imbibe these qualities to make our academic life better. That is why we have to accept the assertion that, knowledge is power. However, I can say without equivocation that, knowledge can only be a powerful tool, if after acquiring these knowledge, it is use judiciously to solve a nagging problem.

Extraordinary students possess setting attributes that make them act beyond the ordinary, the common and the recognized way of doing things. They are seen as outstanding base on their action and results that follows their hard work. Aside that the extend they go, the speed through which they end up achieving remarkable results, makes them exceptional in all their endeavours.

Let us analyse the word extraordinary. The word extraordinary is a combination of two words namely; extra which simply means additional, further and more, whereas, ordinary simply means; normal, usual and common. In short, the extra ordinary student map up strategies, which help them in their quest of achieving their said objective. If you want to standout from your peers and be notice then, you must strive for academic excellence, which is normally associated with the extraordinary students.

Grade "A," are always, the preserve for an extraordinary student because, they spend much of their time doing other things, that will help them position themselves on the higher pedestal, above the ordinary students. Whereas ordinary students are often interested in doing the normal, usual and common which are done by most of their colleagues. This mostly distinguish them from the extraordinary students, who in contrast preferred to do additional studies to further probe into issues, discuss in class. It often helps them to acquire a clear understanding and have an in-depth knowledge of what the teacher taught them. Do you have an extraordinary student in your class? Closely monitor their lifestyle and write the qualities you see in them. After that, modify these qualities to suit your unique persona and soon, you will reach great heights. Once you put them into practise, you will soon become an extra ordinary student.

Who is an extraordinary student?
When we think of extraordinary student, we think of hardworking, student who is smart in getting things done,

by identifying his or her strengths and weaknesses, and focusing mostly on the strength in order to achieve the set objective. You cannot be an extraordinary student and be doing ordinary things. You need to step up your game and yearn for the can do spirit that can energize you to reach the goals and aspirations set out by you. The Twenty-one (21) Qualities of an Extra Ordinary Student that may help turn your life around, are as follows:

1. **They always persevere**

   They have the perseverance spirit, even when things don't seem to be working well they don't through their hands in despair, but continue to press on until they weather the storm. For instance, if they find difficulties in dealing with a subject like Mathematics, they will work around the clock to make sure that they get the understanding, by intelligently surrounding themselves with friends, who understand the topic and learn from them. This make them different from the ordinary, since they always make sure that, any area that they fall short, in their academic pursuit, are carefully tackled, to ensure their continuous stay at the top.

2. **They are self-motivated**

   Most often, extraordinary students are really moved by internal motivations that push them to pursue their dream with little or no external motivations. This kind of motivation, which often comes from within, may spice up their life as they come out enthusiastically to pursue their learning expedition without external influence.

Their self-motivations urge them to believe in themselves and strive for excellence, as they journey their way, through life. In most cases, they know that if they do not take charge of their dream and make it happened no one would do it for them. This alone is enough, to stimulate them to hit the ground running, before someone urges them to do so.

3. **They are confident**

Extraordinary students are always poised for action, this help them to have a positive mindset towards their studies while they forge on, to take the mantle of leadership without been afraid. This give them assurance, that urged them to withstand pressures from people whose agenda is full of arrogance, discouragement and are always ready to kill the can do spirit in them. As they battle with negative minds each day, their confidence help them to overcome these good for nothing words. What keeps them going, as they dare to be extraordinary from their peers, is their confidence.

4. **They are discipline in all their endeavours**

Extraordinary students can restraint or control themselves from any act that will ruin their academic pursuit. With extraordinary students, discipline push them to stay focus, even in the midst of challenges, they do not allow other people's perception to affect them negatively. They rather stay focus and make sure that they maintain the same enthusiasm throughout their studies in order to reach their academic goals.

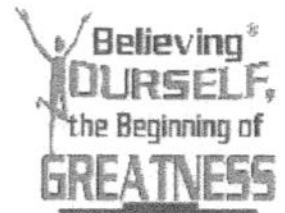

5. They have different mindset

In life everything starts from the mind, as they start their academic journey, their minds are always set on achieving greatness. With this at the back of their mind, they do not settle for lower grades, they set high standard, in their quest of achieving the impossibilities in life. Extraordinary students always go the extra mile in order to be valuable to the environment in which they find themselves. This urges them to move beyond their limit. Since moving beyond their limit, truly define who they are.

6. They don't wait for the right moment but create it themselves

Extraordinary students, always work very hard to create the needed moment that will help them reach the goals and aspirations they have set for themselves in their academic life. Due to this, they set time limits, work within these set periods and make sure that they head towards their set objectives. If their target for the term or semester is to get grade "A" in literature, they make sure that, they use their time wisely and study very hard within the stipulated period to reach their target. After acquiring one set objective, they then long for more, since they know that their plans to greatness are workable.

7. They crave for excellence and dislike mediocrity

Extraordinary students always opt for the best in any career they pursue. When ordinary students get pass sometimes, it seems Ok, but to the extraordinary student, distinction is their ultimate goal, because they hate mediocrity, due to the higher standard they set for themselves. As they continue unabated to crave for excellence, they put aside their mediocre lifestyle, as they set their minds on achieving excellence.

8. They surround themselves with students whose vision is in line with their vision

As the old saying goes, birds of a feather flock together. That is how the extraordinary students behave. They prefer to move with students who are daring to be different and act purposefully in the effort of achieving their goals. In this way, they can influence each other as they forge ahead in their academic life.

9. They study ahead of time

They prepare in advance before classes begins. Most often, before the teacher introduces the topic, they have at least, general overview of it. This gives them, fair idea of the topic under discussion and pave the way for them to ask relevant questions that urges the teacher to elaborate more on the topic, while making the class interactive. As they interact, those who were not clear on the topic may get further explanation. This can broaden their horizon and allow them to benefit from the detailed discussion of the topic, as the teacher's elaboration goes on.

10. They believe in themselves and possess the can do spirit

Once they believe themselves, it will urge them to have a positive attitude, which gives them the needed

passion, to face their academic challenges squarely, without fears. When fearful battle comes their way, their self-believe gives them a top-notch strength to be able to forge ahead and finally achieve their goals.

11. They jot down salient points as and when it becomes necessary

In order to remember some major points, they write down concise note, which sometimes comes off the cuff, as the teacher explains and breaks down the note, for easy comprehension. This helps them to understand the topic in simple and clear terms without any difficulties.

12. They are good listeners

Extraordinary students are good listeners because they listen with rapt attention whenever a teacher is teaching. They concentrate, keep silent and listen in order to get clear information that the teacher wants to send across, without any distortion.

This listening strategy, sustain their interest in every lesson or programme they partake. If you can imbibe this listening approach in your daily conversation and interaction in class, you will always excel in your academic life.

13. They ask questions as and when the need arises

Most of the extraordinary student hates to be timid in class. Due to this, they ask relevant questions to make teaching and learning process lively, interactive and sensational. As they interact, the process helps them to build their self-image, by acquiring skills in communication.

14. They create personal timetable to direct and regulate their studies

To the extraordinary students, time management is essential in their quest of attaining excellent results. Through timetable, they are able to set limit for their friends, who sometimes distract them during their learning activities.

Above all, the timetable also allows them to study each day, in order to make an adequate preparation towards the exams from day one, as school begins. This helps the extraordinary students to avoid the tendency of studying all night a day before the exams, as they prepare for the examination.

15. They always have their dreams and aspirations at the back of their mind

They always look up to the bigger picture and stay resolute as they pursuit their academic goals. Most often, they think about their dreams each day and map up strategies that will guide them, the tactics they need to use and the process that they will follow in order to attain academic excellence. No matter how difficult it is to reach their dreams, they will still persevere until their dreams become reality.

16. They always follow first thing first in their academic life

They know that, the prime objective of every student is to excel in their various areas of study. Moreover,

for them to make an extraordinary progress, they need to take their studies seriously and make a mark in their academic pursuit. Therefore, anything that will obstruct their prime objective is treated as secondary to their academic pursuit.

17. They are prepared to sacrifice everything, to attain academic excellence

They will do everything within their power to attain great heights in their academic pursuit. In reality, they sacrifice their time, resources, and energy to persevere until they reach academic excellence, where the major goals and aspirations they have set for themselves, may be in the full glare of their peers.

18. They always stand out among their peers

They often want to be the best among their peers, so at times they take leadership roles in the class to pave the way for them to stand tall among their peers. As a result, when opportunity comes for them to lead they accept and move on.

When class discussions come, they join with all the needed enthusiasm and lead the discussion. This gives them the charisma to take charge of their own destiny and be notice by others. Gradually, they learn the tenets of leadership, by building their self-confidence and finally, dictating the pace for other students who live ordinary life to follow.

19. They see challenges as an opportunity

They see challenges as a launch pad that can lead them to greatness in their quest for academic excellence. Therefore, when they are faced with task, they always master courage to accept the challenge and execute it to the best of their knowledge. In their quest of finding solution to these challenges, they do further research that helps in broadening their scope of knowledge.

20. They invest in their education

They spend a chunk of their money buying required books and other relevant materials that will help them attain their set objective. For the most part of their lives, they sacrifice food and material happiness and channel most of the resources available for that purposes, towards their education to enable them accomplish their set objectives in no time.

21. They use their leisure period judiciously

Most often, extraordinary students, visit the library during their leisure period to enable them do further research on what the teacher taught them. The research broadens their knowledge and helps them get a clear understanding based on several examples found during the research. These examples make it easier for them to comprehend whatever the teacher taught them and recalled it when the need arises.

Aside that, they love afternoon nap which has been proven by Spanish Society of Primary Care Physicians that, afternoon nap or siesta can reduce pressure or stress, improve alertness and help in the proper functioning of the heart and blood vessels. These stemmed from the fact that, extraordinary people like Albert Einstein, Winston Churchill and

several personalities, are well known nappers who have benefited enormously from napping. You can also experience the benefits that come with afternoon nap, by practicing napping each day with at least from 20 to 25 minutes nap. This will help you de-stress and regain your strength after a hectic day of class activities.

If we acquaint ourselves with the qualities listed above, we will be drawing closer to greatness sooner than we anticipated. That is why daring to be extraordinary as students, can bring success in our academic pursuit. Once you become extra ordinary, it will spark the greatness in you to begin.

Students, who do not dare to be different, mostly accept to mingle with the ordinary student due to that, they do not perform well in the long run. Below are eleven things that lead to students' failure, if they will stay away from it, their quest of achieving greatness will be near.

The rate at which students fail at senior high school level, in recent years, leave much to be desired, that is why, I deem it necessary, touching on the topic, eleven things that lead to students' failure. As eleven (11) major causes of failure in examination at the senior high school level unfold, you will realize the sense of urgency needed for parents, teachers, students and policy makers, to listen and find an antidote, to this disturbing trend. This trend has befall the effort being made by stakeholders in their quest of solving the menace, when you take a cursory look at the performance of the students, you will notice that, there is still more to be done. Have you ever taken pains to look into the root cause of students' failure, if not, then sit down relax, as we go through the study.

1. **Low self-esteem**

Low self-esteem plays a major role in students' failure. It can stop them from taken initiative to learn, believing in themselves and weaken their confidence level. It has the power to reduce average students ability to zero, lessen their thinking ability and finally kill the can do spirit in them. Even when a student knows the answer, he/she still thinks that, a colleague's answer is the right one. It leads to inferiority complex, where they see themselves as nothing and not worthy to pass the exams ahead of them. This may finally give them a failure mentality, thereby pronouncing to them that, they are failures in the battle even before the fight begins.

Low self-esteem can be detrimental to a student quest of passing the summative test, after years of schooling, if is not dealt with properly, their dreams of climbing the academic leather and ascending to the top in their academic pursuit can prove futile.

2. **Lack of perseverance**

Perseverance is crucial, when it comes to life, since life as we perceive, is dynamic not static and is a process, not a one-time destination. Due to this, there are lessons to learnt, hurdles to climb and challenges to be surmounted. Students must not have the notion that, getting grade "A" can be achieved on a silver platter, without putting much effort. They need to step up their learning strategies, do enough research

to find the needed strategies, techniques and tactics that can help them achieve the ultimate. Most often, some do not persevere because, they think they can make it by chance, for the most part of their life, they may be blissfully ignorant of the fact that, chances often comes to an equipped mind that is ready to receive opportunity.

3. **Poor studying skills**

Studying or learning, is a skill that can be learnt to achieve the optimum. Some students are born with the skills already whereas others nurture these skills in order to make it to the top. However, some do not make a conscious effort to seek assistant with regard to tactics, skills and strategies in learning, from their teachers, mentors and colleagues who are endow with these attributes. Nevertheless, they continue to battle with their old ways of learning which do not always yield good result. They finally end up, failing the summative test, which they have spent years preparing.

4. **Focusing on examination leakages**

I can say without equivocation that, examination leakages has led several students to wallop in failure. Most often than not, some of them, do not prepare adequately, because they have the notion that, they will get leakage of the question. As a result, they channel all their effort, looking for leakages without directing their effort towards learning. In view of that, no adequate preparation is done and they end up failing. The crux of the matter is that, most of the examination questions that come out as leakages are fabricated by people to extort money from the students and not necessarily, to help them. In life, effort directed wrongly, can lead to frustration, failure and at times imprisonment.

5. They don't take pains to read the instructions carefully

During the examination, the most important thing to look for is to read the instructions or the rubrics carefully and understand it, before proceeding to answer the questions. What mostly happens is that, some students in the first place, do not take time to intelligently, read the question, and carefully understand it, before providing the right answers. Some of them are not preview to the fact that, passing the exams, mostly rest on, how the individual understand the questions, because understanding the question is part of the exams. On the contrary, if care is not taken and the students deviates the question, the tendency for them to fail is very high.

6. Complacency on the part of students

When complacency engulfs students as flame of fire, they tend to be closed-minded. They then begin to brag and end up, being overconfident without taken pains to prepare adequately, towards impending exams. When the actual examination is due, they tend to struggle because when the question, requires in-depth knowledge, things do not go in their favour. This happens as a result of students been overconfident. As the saying goes too much of

everything is bad. Confidence is good, but been overconfident can let you ignore important details necessary to enable you discuss issues holistically, by providing adequate response to questions that may come your way.

7. **Inadequate learning materials**

If students do not have adequate learning resources such as, class notes, textbooks, and other valuable resources, that can aid them in their preparation towards the exams. When these students proceed to the examination room, to write the exams, the expected outcome may not be good. Assuming in exams you do not have calculator and you are not smart enough to get one from a colleague before the exams begins, your mathematics examination can be detrimental. We all know that, before effective and efficient learning can take place, one needs adequate textbooks and class notes to study in order to prepare adequately towards any examination that may come their way. However, more often than not, some students do not even have these resources to start with. Due to this, the prerequisite knowledge, needed in order to whether the storm during examination, may not be at their disposal. So finally, they may end up losing the battle due to inadequate learning resources.

8. **Misplaced Priorities on the part of students and parents**

If we use the scale of preference, as our measuring line, for measuring our priorities in education, is clear

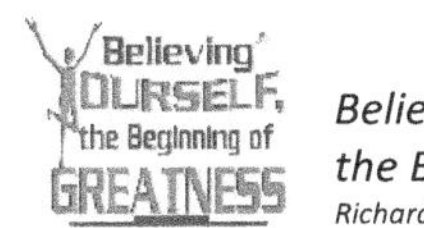

that, our topmost priorities, when it comes to the attainment of educational excellence, are buying of books and other educational resources. Nonetheless majority of students who fail, do not opt for these resources, they rather resort to the buying of material things like sneakers, mobile phones and spend much time playing games and watching irrelevant videos that does not have much bearing on their academic pursuit. As a result, they end up relegating to the background, what really constitute academic excellence. These include textbooks, exercise books, audio, video, and other resources that can augment the effort of the teacher in helping them achieve their goals.

Others also fail, due to the attitude of their parents. They neglect their duties as parent in helping their wards to survive in their quest of attaining academic excellence. Basic necessities that can help shape the child's journey to academic excellence are neglected by some parents based on financial constrain.

Meanwhile, within these constrains, some parents will be living luxurious life that manifest itself in their dressing, the flashy cars they drive, the expensive homes in which they live and the extravagant funeral donations. They do all this, just to impress others, while their ward languished in failure.

9. **Inadequate preparation towards examination**

In order to be a victor in any academic pursuit, there is the need to set goals, and plan ways of achieving

these goals, within a stipulated period. Most often, students prepare, but some of them, their preparations are not adequate to merit good grades. In some cases, they are not able to cover the entire syllabus. Aside that, some students only learn effectively a day to the exams. Once they are not familiar with the content of the subject, they end up finding it difficult to comprehend and recall from memory what they have learnt during the exams. As a result, they then end up failing the summative test after years of schooling.

10. **Relying on colleagues for support, during examination**

Some students are of the notion that, the invigilators will be lenient in the discharge of their duties. If it happens like that, they are sure of getting a colleague student, who will redeem them from the challenges that will befall them, during the exams.

Finally, when the exams begin and the invigilators are strict, their so call dream of passing the exams through the back door will be in vain. Since there will be no room for examination malpractices, failure then becomes inevitable.

11. **Absent from class on several occasions**

Absenteeism can affect the ability for students to comprehend what the teacher taught in their absence. When students absent themselves from class, there is the tendency that, they will resort to a third party for explanation and subsequently copy notes from them.

If the note and explanations by the third parties are wrong, it will definitely affect them negatively.

If you are daring to be different and you fall prey to these eleven things that lead to student's failure, I will entreat you to put these failures behind you and adopt the twenty-one (21) qualities of an extraordinary student. If this is done, your dream of achieving greatness will see the light of day.

Food For Thought

As you dare to be extraordinary, you will learn to believe yourself and stand out from your peers and be notice. When you dare with all the charisma it deserves, you will be toeing the line of greatness. Daring to be extraordinary demands a lot of hard work and perseverance, coupled with other factors, before one can act differently. If reaching the top is an easy task, no one will lag behind, as one craves for greatness. For all you know, it will take extra learning, research, practise and perseverance, to outwit obstacles you will meet in your quest of achieving greatness.

I will entreat you to live a life that often longs to attain new heights. Extra ordinary lifestyle, will gradually dissociate you from friends and acquaintances, since you will be speaking, acting and approaching issues in different manner because you are different. This can happen if you learn to do things differently, by questioning the status quo, while paving the way for creativity to rain as you gravitate towards greatness.

Believing
YOURSELF,
the Beginning of
GREATNESS

"Finding the Right Job That
Takes Cognizance of Your Skills,
Abilities and Interests, Can Save
You From Years of Stress"

Richard Kyere-Boateng

CHAPTER ELEVEN

Finding Job

After years of schooling, skill acquisition and finding a career path, it is now time to look for job opportunities. As you quest for greatness, by battling with life, it will be prudent to opt for one of these two distinct options illustrated below. You can be your own boss, by looking for job opportunities or ideas that can help you start a business on your own.

On the other hand, you can also look for opportunities that can help you get employed in someone else's company. Most often, you will be employed in a place where your services may be needed based on the value you bring on board as an individual. This can augment the effort and measures instilled by the company to enable the company grow from strength to strength.

In the 21st century in which we find ourselves, many research or background checks, are done by myriad of people who wish to venture on their own and employ others in their businesses or seek employment in someone's company where they will be called employees. Finding a new job can be a herculean task in most cases, but once adequate planning is done, you will chance on one. Your plan should take cognizance of the field you want to work, the company you want to work with and the strategy that will help you to get the job. Once planning is done and follow suit, the stress people go through in their quest of seeking job, after several years of schooling, can easily be surmounted. Finding the right job that takes cognizance of your skills, abilities and interests, can save you from years

of stress. So, get your act together and figure out the right job and your life will never be the same. Let us look at the 21st Century skills needed to get employed in any company across the globe.

1. Ability to solve problems

The main purpose of business and institutions is to generate income, through problem solving. For instance, a company may provide the right products or services needed by clients and end up with profit. That is why businesses have interest in recruiting potential problem solvers, who may innovatively identify solutions to problems, as and when it surfaces.

Therefore, having problem solving skills can place you in a more advantageous position, when applying for a job. This can help you stand the test of time, when problems crop up, within your working environment.

2. Ability to work with a team or group

In modern era, most companies are striving hard to leverage in order to spread their businesses to other areas, where potentials in these areas, can be tapped. That is why working together as a team can help the dreams nurtured by these companies materialized.

When a team or group are task to execute a project and they team up with one accord, myriad of ideas, will come from several people, not just an individual. Common mistakes that can easily escape an individual may be identify by the group to ensure the success of the company. If you can coordinate and build a strong team or group, which is formidable enough to withstand the test of time, you will be a pivot within the industry.

3. **Ability to write report**

Our working life is structured in a way that, accounting to people is inevitable once you find yourself in a working environment. Therefore, having the ability to write good and comprehensive report, can take you to places you least expect to be.

The fundamentals in good report writing often stem from observation. Hence, as a writer, you must be able to observe issues, as and when it happens with an eagle eye. This will help you capture most of the essential information, needed during the writing process and be able to give a unique account of what has transpired.

Quite apart from that, you should also take cognizance of the language, whether formal, informal, since using the right vocabulary is crucial to the success of any report an individual writes. If you are a potential employee applying for a job, master these skills to help in your personal development.

4. **Ability to research on new trends**

Every company aims at getting the best product or services, for the consuming public to patronize. That is why companies spend a lot of money, time and effort, researching into ways in which, they can come out with a product or services that can help them stay competitive. It would be a plus for you, if these skills

are captured in your relevant documents as your strength.

5. **Ability to adapt to new situation**

Life in its totality can be equated with the pendulum. This implies that, life as a pendulum can swing back and forth within a short period. Comparatively, a company may also experience dynamic conditions in a twinkling of an eye, which may lead to loss or increase in revenue.

Therefore, having the ability to adopt to new situation or working environment may be crucial to the success of a business as years go by. In life, technology often changes that is why, companies do not often wait for the rippling effect of the change to affect them instead, they rather strategize ahead of time just to meet the ensuing changes.

So mostly, the job description describe in the job you have just applied can change when you finally get employed. That is why companies always look for individuals who can easily adapt to new situations and still fit within the same institution when changes occur. Hence, let your relevant documents and your response during interview exhibit the skill of dynamism.

6. **Ability to manage project**

Managing a project is a skill that any person-seeking job in today's world must possess, since additional skills and abilities are needed, for one to adequately manage a project. Persons having project management skills can perform multi-task and communicate effectively with persons working under them to see any project through.

It can also assist you to develop good negotiating skills, which may be useful when the time comes for you to bargain on behalf of a company and see to the execution of any project. When such time is due, your bargaining skills can bring laurels to the company. Therefore, do all you can within your capacity, to acquire project management skills that will lead you to greatness.

7. **Ability to apply emotional intelligence**

If you have this intelligence, you may be able to work with subordinates and superiors without qualm. Emotional intelligence can help you stay conscious about what is going on in your immediate environment during discussion and give you the power to control your emotions when the need arises. It can also help you to relate well with others at your workplace and enhance your interpersonal skills.

8. **Ability to analyse data**

Data analysis can make significant inroads into a company's quest of achieving greatness. Do you know that, data analysis can pre-inform a company about the exact impact they are making? When data is properly analysed, it can help you do comparative analysis on goods sold or services rendered within a particular year and the previous years to know whether the company is making profit or losses.

Apart from that, comparative analysis can help in adopting a new marketing strategy or maintaining the

old strategy. If any employer gets to know that you can analyse data aside your competencies, you will be the preferred choice among your competitors.

9. Ability to plan and manage organization

As a leader, you are bound to work with several teams or groups, which demand planning, organizing, directing and controlling both human and natural resources to the benefit of the company. These skills when used judiciously can make you a holistic leader. If the company realize that, there is an urgent need for your skills, they will not hesitate by contracting your services. Once you are able to organize, direct and control your subordinate within the company, it will then trigger massive growth.

10. Ability to use the Internet

The power of the Internet cannot be underestimated, since the world is now seen as a global village, so having the ability to access information on the Internet and using search engines to perform a research will raise your competitiveness in the job market.

If you can use social media to send business trending information that will trigger and entice clients and have the skill of performing live conference with Skype and other related application, it will be a plus for you. The Internet will facilitate your work with speed and accuracy in the pursuance of your duties.

On the other hand, if you can send and retrieve information using email, the business will stay on top of current happenings within the globe. If you have these skills, you will be able to use the internet on daily bases, to solve challenges that will crop up without much difficulty.

Things to consider when creating your own business

Many people want to be their own boss, but to be your own boss, mostly come with a considerable price that you need to pay, in order to sustain and grow the business from a small beginning to greater achievement. These prices include discipline, perseverance, initiative, adventure, risk and many more.

The benefit that comes with the formation of your own business, are enormous, since the turnover you will accrue, is often hundred percent. This amount will usually come to you, after paying few subordinates, whom you are leveraging to see the expansion of your business, from small to medium scale. If this is your dream, then you are an entrepreneur.

What an entrepreneur does is they look for opportunities by carefully analysing the environment, finding what is lacking and undertaking a risk to provide these needs to maximize profit. Below are some of the few things needed to enable you start your own business and reach great heights.

1. **Have the dream of starting something**

    Entrepreneur's vision, mission and strategies often begin in the mind as mental pictures. These pictures may represent the dream he/she want to pursuit as they begin their journey to the world of commerce. When the picture surfaces, there may be several

images, but the onus rest on you, to select the feasible one that you are passionate about. Once your passion is at work, you will never forsake this dream, until a resounding success is achieved.

2. Document your plan

The plan or strategy must be documented for easy comprehension. This will allow the entrepreneur to refer, modify and strategize for the near future. When ideas are documented, it can move from generation to generation, without losing its value. If your idea is worth supporting, various financial institutions, friends and family members who wish to support the idea may do so without qualm. For example, if you have a plan that is documented and contains the objectives, strategies and tactics to complete a specific project, seeking financial support to see the plan through, will not be any difficult hurdle.

3. Start as low as the little you have

In business, is good to have huge capital, but if the said amount is not there, you must be able to think in a creative manner by acting in a more resourceful way. Thinking outside the box can stretch your imagination to discover things that can stimulate your vision to come to fruition. This can be done innovatively, when you start with what you have. If you start with what you have and there is a risk, it will not be too risky, as compared to paying debt from the bank.

What you have, means a lot, it can represent the ideas you possess, the time you have, the interest that drives you, and the network of influential friends at your disposal. These are your immediate resource base that can support the ideas you have in kind or cash to start without much risk. If your resources are limited, the easiest field you can venture is services. Most often, you can start with little capital. However, for stock, mostly huge capital is needed to buy the initial goods or materials to fill the shop. That is why it would be prudent to think through your decision whether to go for stock or services before hitting the ground running.

4. **Seek assistance from a role model who is working in the field you want to venture**

You can seek first-hand assistance from your role model, to enable you acquaint yourself with the rules of the game. The experience you will accrue from your role model will help you make an informed decision that may save you years of trial and error.
This decision can be a game changer that can turn your life around by directing your steps in your journey to entrepreneurship.

5. **Be prepare to pay the price**

In order to stay competitive and see your business blossoming among other businesses, you will need a perseverance spirit, a discipline mindset and adventurous character, to see greatness in your life.

Discipline will be your normal lifestyle, once you focus on the bigger picture you are longing to achieve. Due to this, you will discipline yourself to enable you surmount any obstacle that stands between you and

greatness. It will then give you the needed effort to persevere, by channelling all your effort towards that go. Your colleagues will then see you as a person, who takes initiative often. This will ignite the adventurous nature in you and as a result, you will no longer see risk taken as a daunting task, but a step towards your goals and aspirations.

Things to consider when looking for job

Is not everyone who can run a successful business immediately after graduating from a tertiary institution. With some people they have to work, be closely monitored, supervised, acquired the experience and gradually build their self-confidence, before they can kick-start their own business, later in life. That is why majority of graduates, deem it prudent to search for job, immediately after graduating. Therefore, what goes into your curriculum vitae (CV) and other relevant documents, must be carefully examined before applying for the job. I will entreat you to consider the steps listed below, when the time comes for you to find job.

1. **Know the type of company or institution you want to work with**

   You must do a background check about the company you want to work with, before sending your application letter. Basic information like, company name, type of businesses they do, whether they are into education, manufacturing or services. This may be relevant during the interview, in case a related question is posed to you.

2. Know the position, you want to apply

Be specific as you can, when dealing with job opportunities. You must know the type of position you wish to apply and the role you will be playing in regard to the job. Then inform the friends you had in college, internship, mentoring and close friends you have built over the years. They are the network of people, who can assist you to get the position or vacancy you have been longing for. Their role is to connect you to influential friends they know, who may cause positive changes to happen in your life, which may take you to greater heights.

For the most part of your job search, this crop of people may serve as a liaison, by linking you to vacancies available within your grasps. Therefore, being specific can clear the ambiguity in the minds of people who wants to recommend you. This can easily be done when you take time to strategize, as you think through several positions available, before applying for the job.

3. The skill set you possess

You must highlight the skill sets you are bringing to the company. These set of skills may in one way or the other, impact positively on the performance of the company. If the skills you are highlighting in your curriculum vitae are not related to the skill set needed by the employer to fill the vacant position, then you may be striving for success, but your effort may not yield any good returns. Therefore, I will entreat you as job seeker, to match your skill sets, with the

position you are applying. Quite apart from that, you must demonstrate how skilful you are, by applying the knowledge you have accrued over the years to solve a problem that comes before you, as you launch a search to find a job. This will allow you to stay competitive and in the end, pave the way for you to be slated for interview.

4. Your interest

In life, if you work within an environment or company you are not passionate about, mostly your performance will never go beyond average.

However, if you are holding a certain position or working within a company where your passion drives you, mostly your performance will range from above average to excellence.

Aside that, the ideas you have, may flow smoothly, without much impediments because the job you are embarking on, may finally be a hobby, when in reality is a job. That is why it is always good to consider your interest before making moves to find job. Once you have the passion or interest for the job, you will surely find fulfilment in it.

5. Can the job put food on your table?

You must do a background check, to find out whether, the job you are applying, the salary you will accrue during payday, can put food on your table. This must be done first before, allowing the joy of getting employment control your mind and sway you to succumb to what will bring regret to you, for not finding out the amount involved. This does not mean you should go directly and ask for the salary package that comes with the job, but it can be done indirectly through a third party. In some cases, the remuneration associated with the job is captured in the job adverts. Therefore, when you are reading a job advert, open your eyes and observe little details that can make-or-break you as a worker.

6. **Leverage others to see your dream through**

When it comes to job seeking, no matter who you are, you need the support of others, to see your dream materialized. If you take the network of friends you have from college, internship, national service and religious organizations, they can be a huge asset through which you can get employment. For all you know, your friend may know someone and that person may know others who can be of help to you in your job search.

Five simple ways of finding a job

In life, individuals can find the job they are looking for, in several ways without sweating their guts out, once they follow the five areas discussed below.

1. **Network**

You must build a network of influential personalities who can recommend you in times of need. They will come handy when the time comes for you to look for employment. All you need to do is to pre-inform them about your intention to look for job. They will then take it from there, by connecting you to a group of influential people within their network. Sooner rather

than later, they will liaise you to a company and you will be employed.

2. Recommendations

Through recommendation, several people get employed each day. When the opportunity comes for you to work, just put in your best in every job related task that comes your way.

Do you know that people you least expect in life, can recommend you directly and indirectly without you knowing it. Therefore, never underestimate the power of recommendations and always try as much as possible to live a mark in others minds that will merit recommendations, when the need arises. In short, you will merit recommendation from people once you build a good rapport with them.

3. Website and social media

In the 21st century in which we find ourselves, social media, blogs and websites cannot be underestimated with regard to business. Chunk of information, flow through them each second, minute and hour as each day goes by. In recent years, most job openings are corresponded regularly through the internet. Vacancies are advertised, for prospective applicants to apply by submitting their application, CV and relevant documents online, through emails and third party software, to get employed.

If you are ignorant of the World Wide Web and its social media platforms, such as LinkedIn, Twitter, Instagram, Facebook, then learn to adopt to it because it is the easiest platform through which people can find job vacancies.

4. Internship

When you get opportunity to listen to a cross section of workers, a reasonable number of them got employ through their internship programme. It all boils down to the fact that, during their internship, they worked assiduously and as a result, their employers were impress and later shown interest in employing their services after graduating.

Bear in mind that when opportunity comes for you to exhibit your skills and interest, during internship or national service, do not portray lackadaisical attitude towards work. Just work assiduously for all you know, your effort will not be in vain. Since your boss will be watching you from a distance without you knowing it, put in your best and your best will pave a way for you.

On the contrary, if you allow lackadaisical attitude to overshadow your life within the company, the chances of you getting employed by them will be slim, when the service or internship is over. For all you know, you will be living under the illusion that, you will get employed when in reality your employee sees you as a liability to the company. So let your action, motives and attitude, portray the lifestyle of a determine and hardworking person, who will always go an extra mile, to reach his/her goals and aspirations.

5. Recruitment Agencies

In recent years, looking for job has taken a new twist, which involves third parties. There have been a lot of companies whose core purpose is to link employee seeking job, to employers looking for employees.

Therefore, if you find yourself in any difficulties trying to lay your hands on a job, do not worry your redeemer is here. Recruitment agencies have come now to help you, in your quest of getting employed. Your role is to look for these agencies and submit an application through their noble office, to enable them link you to the right job.

Things to consider when applying for a job

When the time is due to apply for job vacancies, you must take note of the following ideas listed below to enable your goals and aspirations come true without much sweat.

1. Look for the minimum requirements

If you do not want to be disqualified, when you are applying for a job, always look at the minimum requirements that comes with the job vacancy. It will further inform you whether you qualified for the job or not. Basic information that are often required includes age limit, minimum qualification, sex whether female or male and many more.

For instants, if the job you are applying requires a female to perform a specific task that is female oriented, a male cannot apply. If you are a male and your application finds its way to the company, it will not be considered. On the other hand, if both sex are required, both can apply without any restrictions.

2.   Your application must have goals

In life we find ourselves, goal setting cannot be separated from achievement. The application that will market you, must be goal oriented. This will help send a strong signal to the employer that you have something up your sleeves. If they realized that, your goals could turn the fortunes of the company around, you will be shortlisted and subsequently called for an interview. Therefore, take your time and make sure that the goals you have set in your application letter, is in line with the company's goals in totality. When this is done, it will clear all ambiguity, which surrounds the understanding of your application during perusal.

3.   Cover letter (Covering letter)

Cover letter can open a door of opportunity for you to be called for interview. On the other hand, it can also close your chances of qualifying you for an interview and subsequently getting employment, if it is not properly written.

Remember your cover letter can speak volumes of you, in your absence. Your cover letter must introduce you to the employer, justify why you are the best person for the job and in addition touch on few things your curriculum vital (CV) could not describe.

It should also specify the area you want to work within the company and finally qualify you for interview.

4. **Curriculum Vital (CV)**

Your CV must be chronologically arrange to ensure easy perusal. When your CV's are arranged in an orderly manner that takes cognizant of various categories like, educational background, working experience and skills, it will certainly sustain the interest of your potential employer.

Take note that the current crop of CV's has two pages for applicants who have working experience, whereas a single page CV is recommended for a fresh graduate who doesn't have much working experiences, but have been on internship. This has been necessitated as a result of time and its essence to the employer, since numerous applications and CV's are often sort out before candidate are shortlisted. So gone are the days when applicants use to write and send copious CV's to employers, which previously ranges from five to eight pages.

Try as much as possible to eliminate blemishes, elaboration and stay with brevity. Always let this catch phrase guide you, keep it simple, concise and straight to the point.

5. **A Portfolio of related works**

If the job description demands that, you will execute works of that nature in your line of duty, then it may be a plus for you to build a portfolio of related works if possible, to highlight your practical skills to your potential employer.

When you meticulously build a portfolio, it may speak volumes of the practical experiences you have built overtime and gradually, your hands on experience may be seen during perusal. So, put in your best when designing your portfolio to show the practical side of you, to your potential employer.

Things to consider when you are called for interview

Before attending any interview, you must prepare adequately ahead of time, to enable you respond well to various questions that may come your way. Do you know that if you are called for an interview, most often you may be part of shortlisted candidates especially, when the applicants are many? Once you are shortlisted, you may be few steps away from being employed.

For the most part of your job search, your curriculum vitae can help in the advancement of your career, which mostly comes with huge monitory gains. You must ask yourself few rhetorical questions to help you stay on point. Do my personality and skillset, matches the information found on my curriculum vitae (CV) or cover letter? Am I ready to work within an environment of this nature?

Below are things to consider when you are attending an interview. It has been categorized into three stages namely: before, during and after the interview.

Before the interview
Before the interview takes place, one needs to familiarise him/herself with the things that will help him/her pass the interview.

1. **Time conscious is crucial**

   Being time conscious, speaks volume, about how reliable you are when it comes to work. If time is of great essence to you, at least, you must be able to reach the interview centre, fifteen minutes before the

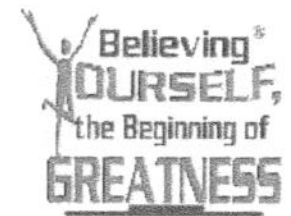

interview starts. This will offer you the opportunity, to relax and release any tensions that will surface because of lateness.

2. Inform the receptionist officially

On arrival see the receptionist and announce your presence. This can be done by introducing yourself officially to the receptionist in clear statement by mentioning your name and purpose. By doing so, your name will be added to the current list of interviewees readily available, to be interviewed. After that, you then wait patiently to be interviewed, as soon as it reaches your turn.

3. Be well informed about the company

You must keep abreast of current happenings within the company. For instance, the name of the company, the activities they do, their target audience, where they are and where they want to be in the foreseeable future. Aside that, you must be well informed about the job you are applying and the responsibilities associated with the position. This will give you, the prerequisite knowledge, needed to have a competitive urge when the interview kicks off. If you are fortunate to be posed with related questions, based on the research you have done about the company, the probability of passing the interview will be very high.

4. Prepared adequately

Adequate preparation is vital for individuals to attain success when it comes to interview. Therefore, as an interviewee, prior preparation should not be overlooked. A holistic preparation that takes into consideration of the writing of a CV, research, rehearsals and time of the interview must be of paramount importance to you, if you really want to be a victor. Once you are fully prepared, all your effort would be in the full glare of the interviewers when the planning becomes effective and efficient. For the most part of your life, just embrace preparation and let it be your hallmark as you journey towards greatness.

5. **Likely interview questions**

As the day of the interview draws nearer, you can take note of the trending questions that interviewees faces most often when they attend interviews and master them to ensure victory on the said day. As you crave for greatness, it will be prudent on your part to stay alert with the current crop of questions that interviewers often ask interviewees. Being preview to these likely questions can galvanized you into action, as you aspire to new heights. Below are samples of trending interview questions and their responses.

   i. **Tell us about yourself?**

Tell us about yourself is sometime framed as run us through your curriculum vitae. The question demands you to touch on your educational background, your skill set and its relevance to the position you are applying. Most often than not, the interviewers will be looking for clues like, how confident and passionate you respond to issues and your command over the language where applicable. The educational background

refers to the knowledge you have accrued, through college, if possible mention the college. About your skills, you can touch on your previous working life or internship you had with a firm and the skills you gain during the said period.

The crux of the matter is that, all that you have said in relation to your education, skill and experience must be relevant to the job you are applying. If your education, skills and experience have a direct link to the said position or job, then you have already made an impressive beginning.

ii. **Why do you want to join us?**

What this question demands of you is to affirm all the good skills, abilities and interest you said you possessed. They want you to convince them, why you think you can fit within the house style of the company. You must be able to link the qualities you possess and its direct relations to the house style of the company by demonstrating how your skills, interest and abilities match the job in perspective.

In short, the panellist wants to know whether you know much about the company. For instance, their core values, business culture and the achievements they have made so far. If you have them at your fingertips, you can then respond accordingly.

iii. **Why do you think we should hire you?**

What this question demands is to sell yourself in front of them, aside the CV and other relevant documents. You can easily answer this question, if you know the job description by heart. You can relate your skill set to the job description. For instance, if you have any history of major differences that your skill set has made in your previous working life do not be afraid to voice it out when the need arises. When your answer is in tandem with why they are hiring you, then soon you will reach great heights.

iv. **What is your greatest weakness?**

Is all about identifying the weaknesses you have aside your strength, while you outline ways to fix them. If you are smart enough, you can first touch on something that you are doing great, but fall short in some aspect of it. It all boils down to the fact that there are some areas you are still learning in order to perfect your skill in that small part of a whole. For example if your job demands the knowledge of "Microsoft Office Suite", you can highlight where you are good at and where you need to make conscious effort to bring to perfection.

In short, you say, I have command over Word, Excel and PowerPoint but when it comes to access, I only know the basics, and I promise to learn beyond the basics to stay competitive by the time I get the job. This response, may pre inform the panellist that, you are making conscious effort to fix the flaws in your life.

v. **Where do you want to be in five years' time?**

This question is meant to find out whether you have plans of leaving the company after five years

or if you are hired, you will be available to ensure that, the company moves from strength to strength.

In response, you can stress on the fact that, you have what it takes to build a strong team, formidable enough to take the company to places. Let them know that, you would coordinate with the subordinates to ensure that, in five years' time, there will be several branches to augment effort of the main branch. This will help the company in its quest to attain the strategic plan, they have envisage, in five years' time.

6. Dress code, keep it simple, but formal

When it comes to attending an interview, dress code is strictly formal, so bear in mind and follow it. Avoid extravagant dressing and keep it simple. Remember the interview room is not a designated place you can dressed to kill. So keep it simple with a colour scheme that is not too hot. A well-ironed dress will say a lot about your attention to details and give you a presentable look that will resonate with the interviewers.

7. Let your body smell good

In recent years, most of the room designated for interviews, are fully air-conditioned. Therefore, it will be in your own interest, to smell good to prevent, the panellist from disqualifying you from getting the job, due to body odour. Deodorant or body spray can tone down the body odour, to enable you respond

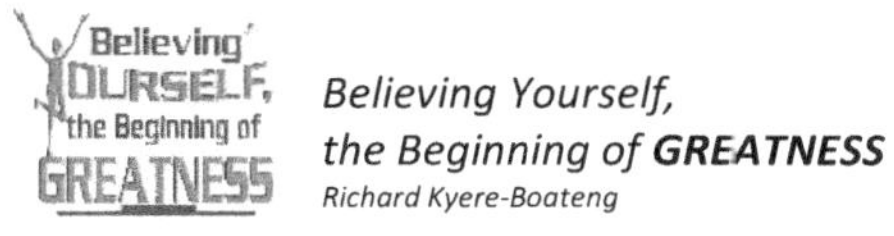

adequately, to questions with all the confidence it needs, without losing your dignity.

8. **Be aware of the place of the interview**

Before the day of the interview, it will be in your own interest, to visit the place where the interview will be done, it possible. Once you visit the place, you will be able to acquaint yourself with the environment and the direction to the designated location where the interview will be conducted.

In contrast, if there are not enough resources to do so or the distance to the place will take several hours, you can ask for directions to the place. Apart from that, it would also be prudent to find out the time, minutes and the hours that will take you before reaching the place. You must find out the amount needed to ply the route, so that you can make provision towards it, when the time is due.

9. **Be aware of the date of the interview**

The exact date of the interview must be at the back of your mind, as each day passes. Write it in your diary, set alarm to remind yourself of it. Once the alarm rungs, it will serve as a reminder. On the other hand, as you flip through your dairy each day, it will then keep you abreast with appointments that are yet to be honoured. You then honour this appointment when the schedule date is due.

10. **Bear in mind that, interview can take any form**

When you are as to attend an interview, it can take any form such as written, oral and practical. So do not

have the notion that interview is only oral. You can be asked to write, written interview, this is where interviewees answer theory questions on paper.

When it is oral, the interviewers will often, interact with interviewees. Aside that, interview can also be practical, where your hands on experience are subject to critical analysis. I will entreat you to find out the kind of interview, you are attending to enable you, prepared adequately towards that.

11. **Greet the panellist**

Before the interview begins, when you are called to enter, knock where necessary and greet the panellist. You then wait to be offered a seat, before proceeding to sit down. Remember not to cross your legs, for its offensive in some cultures, to do so in front of dignitaries.

As you face the panellist, it will be prudent on your part not to sit in any posture that depict reclining, but sit in a manner that suggest that you are eager and prepared to respond to questions set before you.

During the interview
When the interview begins, there are myriad of things that an interviewee can do, in order to get the position or job. When these steps are followed to the later can bring a resounding victory to the interviewee. Study them and adjust yourself to ensure victory at the end of the interview.

1. **Be honest in your response**

When the interview begins, just be honest as possible and relate your responses to information captured in your cover letter, CV and other relevant documents, presented to the interviewers. In short, your curriculum vital and your response must be in harmony, in other to win their trust. If at any point in time if it is out of sync with your relevant documents, they will lose trust in you. If it happens like that, the least said the better.

2. **Your response must be concise**

Your response to questions asked by the interviewers should be as brief as possible. If your answer is yes or no at any point in time, a brief explanation must follow through. Let brevity guide your response, in order to stay within the confines of your question, to avoid going overboard.

The crux of the matter is that, your answer must carry all the information needed to respond adequately in a short possible way.

3. **Don't show sign of disrespect to your previous employer**

No matter how bad, you were treated in your previous job, when a question is posed to you, about why you left the company, do not follow your emotions and respond in a derogatory way, thinking that, it will prompt them to favour you.

You must do your best and respond adequately to the question, without any emotional sentiments. You can further touch on facts that necessitated your resignation and stay within that context without going overboard.

4. Make good use of eye contact

To be able to build and maintain your confidence throughout the interview, eye contact cannot be under estimated.

Most often than not, eye contact will bring out the boldness in you and keep you abreast of the next question as you study the body language of the interviewers and respond accordingly. It will help you stay focus, attentive and vigilant throughout the interview to avoid missing the mark when questions are pose to you.

5. When given the opportunity to ask question, accept and respond

Before the interview ends, if a question comes to you, like do you have any question to ask the panellist? Do not be in a hurry to say no, you must see it as an excellent opportunity to ask a question that relates to the position you want to occupy.

You can ask a question to clear a doubt going through your mind. The question you will pose should not be a mere question, but a well thought of question that will send a signal to the interviewers that, you are the best person for the job.

After the interview

When the interview is over, several things can be done, in order to catch the attention of the panellist. At times these can somehow make-or-break the interviewee quest to reach greatness.

1. **Thank the interviewers**

When the interview ends, thank the panellist. Be brief as possible, by expressing hope of hearing from them soon with a polite smile, while you leave quietly. This will display a reciprocity of respect between the interviewers and the interviewees.

In some cultures, the panel can be pleased only with a thank you note, if possible the same day. They see a thank you note as a formal way of thanking the panellists for the audience granted you. It can be in a form of a physical card or soft copy design send through email. Your thank you note should be well crafted and must be devoid of grammatical errors in order to make an impact.

2. **Justified your inclusion when you get the job**

When you are privileged, to be offered the position, you applied, count yourself lucky. Right from day one, you must exhibit the character trait that made them to select you as a preferred choice.

Do you know that, applicants who came for the interview were equally good candidates who competed fervently with you for the job, but were not selected? If by any point in time, you fail to perform your duties according to their expectation, they may think, they made mistake by selecting you.

If you allow your non-performance to trigger negativity in their mind, you will never find fulfilment in that working environment. So, do all you can by working assiduously for the company to know that, you got the job through competitive selection.

3. Bring to bear your extraordinary skills

From day one, you must be prepared to display the extraordinary skills and abilities you possessed. If you do, it will go a long way to make a greater impact in the new working environment in which you find yourself. This different skill set will separate you from the ordinary colleague at your work place. Your extraordinary skills will be a trumped card that will salvage the company in times of need. So put in your best skills you can ever think of, to ensure that, your credibility and your expertise takes the business to a new heights.

4. Make your presence felt

When priority is giving to you to work in a new position, all eyes will be on you. A lot of staff will be monitoring your progress from time to time. It will be in your own interest to make your presence felt, by solving major challenges. This will gradually prepare you towards a higher pursuit, which can be in a form of promotion.

5. Work towards great heights

In your working life, you can opt for what others have done and pursuit that average agenda, but if you really want to distinguish yourself, then you need to think, act and yearn for exceptional qualities, the can aid you to reach new heights.

Staff who work towards great heights, often found innovative ways of solving problems as and when it appears. This makes them genius in where ever they find themselves.

How to secure your job and enjoy your working life

Good Job that pays well, is hard to come by, in the same vein, is not everyone who will get a better job that comes with a lucrative income, at the beginning of a working life. Therefore, when you are counted among the elite in society, due to the lucrative job you have gotten, do whatever is legally and morally right to secure yourself in order to avert losing the job that has brought major changes in your life. Below are few ideas that can help you in the quest of securing your job, to enable you experience its benefits, time after time. They are as follows:

1. **Learn to work with others**

   To make a significant gain within your working vicinity, you must learn to relate well with both subordinates and superiors. Since your progress and your downfall can be influenced by their actions and inactions, let that cordiality exist.

   You must bear in mind that, they can recommend you by affirming you or they can report you based on something you are not doing right. Besides, if they harbour secret grudge against you, it will spelt doom for you, if it not well managed. Relating well with a colleague worker, either superior or subordinate, may speak volumes of your coordination and cohesive skills that may lead you to places.

2. **Respect your superiors**

   Most often, their decisions come make-or-break your job. As you liaise with them, do not offend them with your utterances or body language. This does not mean

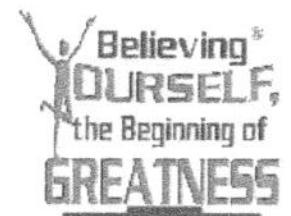

that, you should keep silent or sit aloof if the company is infringing on your write, No, it means be bold and channel your grievances, through the right processes and procedures.

In this way, your boss may not like your submissions, but he will not equate you to an insolent person. Due process will hide your physical emotions and body language that often breeds intemperate words. Respecting your superior does not mean that, you should pander to his/her wrong doings, but abide by the code of ethics of the job, by upholding and defending it, when the need arises.

3. Avoid gossiping

If you always eavesdrop or gossip about your own colleagues, one day it may land you in a complete chaos that can bring shame and distrust to you within your working vicinity. The people you are gossiping with can turn against you, so be vigilant.

During gossiping, if you leave them to attend to any other duty, you will be the next suitable subject for these gossipers. At times, gossipers may be spies contracted to investigate you indirectly to know how you relate to your boss. Gossipers end up thinking negatively about others instead of analysing their own shortcomings and finding ways of fixing these flaws of theirs.

Therefore, lazing around during working hours and gossiping about others can land you into trouble one day. If gossiping has been your hobby, I will entreat you to wise up and deal with problems directly to avert trouble. Instead of gossiping, you can use that time judiciously, by learning additional skills that may add extra value to yourself, if you really want to achieve greatness.

4. Learn from hard working staff

If by any means, you chance on someone who is hardworking and dedicated to duty, within the workplace, you can learn from him/her to enable you instil some of the qualities the person possesses. When you are exposed to their influential lifestyle over a period, it will shape your attitude towards work, transform your life at the workplace, and finally trigger your greatness to begin.

5. Learn not to apportion blame

Try as much as you can, to avoid blame game when trouble crops up. Blame game will often suggest that you are pandering to the whims of others. No matter how persuasive or debilitating their actions and inactions has landed you, stay focus.

If you don't stop this barbaric act, you will be channelling your energy towards blaming others, instead of taking steps to reach greatness.

In life, if you really want to stay focus and reach greatness in no time, then be responsible for decisions or choices you have made and when failure comes because of indecisions, accept, apologized and move on.

Blaming others cannot aid you to make progress in life but it will rather belittle you and finally bring chaos and confusion that will frustrate you to give up on what you are doing.

6. **Work each day as if you own the business**

When premium is placed on tasks you execute daily, with all the sense of agency it deserves, as if is your own job, the business will grow and you will soon benefit from your labour. It will urge you to work assiduously with a professional touch to ensure that, your output is often the best. Once you tackle each work with this mindset, you will gradually set a standard that will help the business reach new heights.

When your role in the business becomes indispensable, your dream of securing of job will come to fruition. As your hardworking character traits become visible to your superiors and subordinates, some subordinates will quickly discourage you with the notion that is not your business, why are you killing yourself for a job that is not yours. The onus is on you to ignore their comments and move on.

Your major greatness begins when you start working, if you are lucky, you may begin with a lucrative job. Only few people begin their working life in such a rosy, cosy and juicy way. Precious one, do not think that, your road to greatness will be a life of ease, no! That is why you have to, safeguard your job by working assiduously, wherever you find yourself, to enable you, stay effective and efficient in each task that comes your way.

Aside that, you must always work with good intention towards whatever job your hands finds. Who knows, others may be monitoring you from a distance, to recommend you for a better job opportunity, when the need arises.

Food For Thought

Finding the right job can set an individual free from the shackles of poverty and catapult him or her to greatness. As we all know, success cannot be achieve on a silver platter, you have to work for it.

In the 21st century in which we found ourselves, the job field has been very competitive. Since the number of students graduating each year far outweighs the number of jobs available, do your utmost best. When you start adding value to yourself academically or practically, you will soon gain a competitive advantage over your acquaintances.

Have you ever assess how competitive you are to your fellow students, job seekers and acquaintances. Aside your area of expertise, what additional qualities can qualify you as the best person for the job?

There are basic tools and ideas that the 21st century students, graduates and workers can learn in order to be different from the rest. For instance, how to use the search engine to do basic research, how to enter and analyse simple data, how to plan and manage projects on your own, how to send and retrieve emails and how to write comprehensive report.

You will certainly bear with me that, if someone has these as an additional skills and he/she is your competitor applying for the same job, the least said the better. Therefore, wake up from your slumber and acquaint yourself with these skills to enable you acquire a competitive edge in your quest for greatness.

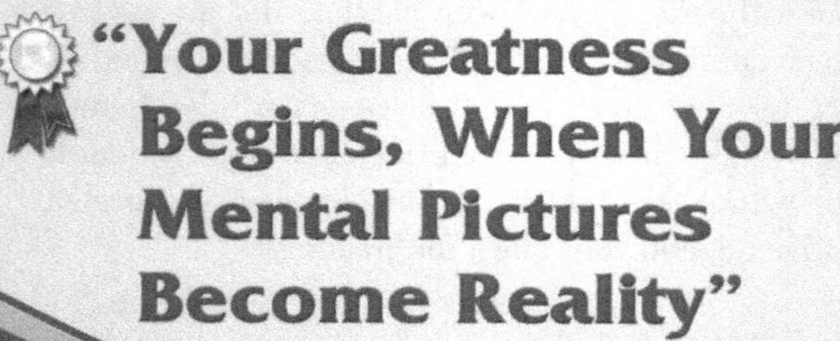
"Your Greatness Begins, When Your Mental Pictures Become Reality"
Richard Kyere-Boateng

Believing
YOURSELF,
the Beginning of
GREATNESS

CHAPTER TWELVE

Your Greatness Begins

Most people want to be great, but are not keen on finding out, what really constitute greatness. If you achieve something that seems to be above what an average person can achieve, it is seen as greatness. Many people became great, by going the extra mile in whatever they set their minds on. At times, the extent they go, their endurance, perseverance and the spirit that drive them, coupled with the influence they make, often place them above an average person.

If it is your wish to be great, that is not enough, because wishes alone cannot create greatness. It takes the power of self-believe, conscious effort and a perseverance spirit to attain greatness. If you consistently apply these principles over a period of time, you will soon step into greatness, without you knowing it. Eventually, you will reach the destination you have set for yourself, before your hour of greatness tick away.

After knowing your career path and finally get employed, you can then toe the line of greatness and be great in no time. If I may ask, what is greatness? Greatness is the ability to turn your abilities into reality, which may have a positive influence on others' live that, will finally bring fulfilment. This can be attain through your words, actions and emotions. In short, greatness is all about positive influence. Great people, always long for excellence to enable them position themselves well, in order to

influence others in a positive way. If your success story is having great impact on people living within your community, your country and the world as a whole, then you are heading towards greatness.

Mostly, greatness does not come on a silver platter, unless you work for it. Almost all those who achieved greatness, in their chosen career or endeavours often had some exceptional qualities that made them great. Your greatness begins, when your mental pictures become reality. Therefore, live a lifestyle that will tilt your focus towards greatness and finally make you great.

Below are some attributes that can spark the greatness in you to begin.

1. **Have a definite plan**

Having a definite plan in mind, is the first step to greatness. A definite plan or purpose is a cardinal step that defines the strategies needed to achieve your goals and aspirations. As you set your goals, do not focus too much at your current state, but start by focusing on where you want to be. With these ideas, and abilities in mind, greatness can come your way. That is why, when great ideas start surfacing in your mind, the onus is on you, not to write them off, based on financial constraints or your present location. If you make a mistake and limit these great ideas, stemming from your mind, owing to the fact that it is not achievable, at that particular moment, then your plan will flop. If you are not careful, you may end up truncating brilliant ideas that may have tremendous impact in your life that will finally impact positively, on the lives of many people.

After setting your goals, you need to strategize on what you want to do in order to achieve your purpose. Next is to plan the strategies that will help you in your quest of achieving your goals and aspirations. You must instil measures that will enforce the systems and processes you will follow each day, in order to reach your purpose. Then after the systems and processes, you then decide on the task you will perform each day, to enable you reach the target you have set for yourself.

Planning is the foundation on which several framework emanates from. In order to achieve greatness, planning take cognizance of the fact that, any dream that comes from the mind of an individual, must be documented. Planning will mostly capture the timelines for achieving the objectives you have in mind, to avert the tendency of losing it for good. If you allow planning to dominate all stages in your life as you journey to greatness, you will be able to confront any obstacle that may come your way. From that moment, the defeatist may wonder how you did it.

2. Focus your mind toward greater pursuit

You must tune your mind to have the mindset of great people, in your journey to greatness. Great minds, defy the odds that come their way as they forge ahead in life. Most often, they focus their mind primarily towards their goals without looking back.

Great people are not oblivious to the fact that, greatness begins from the mind. That is why they always feed their mind with the necessary information, needed to enable them reach their goals

and aspirations. Deep within them, they know that greatness can be pursued, once individuals focus on ways of shaping their mindset. After shaping their mindset, it will stimulate them to hit the ground running by implementing their plans.

3. You will begin to act like a great person

The way you think, look, and feel will be an exact replica of a great mind. As your actions get influenced day in and day out by great ideas, arising from, a change of mindset, it will lead you to places. When you start believing yourself, the change you will experience will be great enough to place you on a higher pedestal. Your words, actions and emotions will portray the lifestyle of a great mind who is yearning to achieve greatness.

Your greatness begins when your mental pictures become reality. When such time comes, take note of events and appreciate the changes that follows suit, by adjusting your lifestyle accordingly to fit your new status quo, when the need arises. You will now be addicted to the positive lifestyle of the optimist, who often perceives issues with optimism. The optimistic nature you have adopted will tilt your focus and actions in a positive direction that will gradually lead you in a steady pace into the kingdom of greatness.

4. You will identify opportunities, in limited situations

As the mindset of greatness engulfs you as an individual, you will see greatness in most of the challenges you encounter each day and overcome them. Due to your fervent quest for greatness, you will continue to press on, until you reach your set objectives. Even if you encounter challenges, your mind will fish out, some good lessons from it, which will equip you to face life head on. These lessons will then assist you to see a window of opportunity within any challenging moments, which may come your way. This ingenuity happens to those who have open mindset that tilt their action towards greater pursuit.

When your believing power reaches its pinnacle, you will be seeing solutions in most of the challenges that will confront you. Since you have antidote to myriad of challenges that may crop up within these period, you will not bedevilled by self-doubt, but you will rather be filled with self-believe, which will finally lead you to greatness. The self-believe imbibed in you, will often urge you to identify solutions in limited situations, since you have the mindset of great people.

5. Your can do spirit will shot up

Once you tune your mind towards greatness, it will be difficult for someone to stop you from pursuing your goals. For the most part of your life, once your spirit shot up, it will urge you to believe yourself. As a result, when others are struggling to take initiative, you will see taken initiative, as a daily routine for the great mind.

Relenting in your effort, will no longer be a strategy that will drive you towards life but your believing power. This power will always be a motivating factor that will lead you to greatness.

6. Take Action

Great people often take initiative that turns the wonderful ideas they have nurtured over the years, into achievable goals. For the most part of great people's life, they follow their lifetime dreams from the planning, implementation and finally, at the supervisory stages, until their dreams happen. They know deep within their minds that, when they take initiative, it will not be rosy at the early stages, but once they learn from their mistakes each day, they will have the cutting edge in fixing any anomalies that may confront their actions. This often inspire them to take action that will enable the dreams and aspirations, they have in mind, become a reality. Later on, those who thought they were daydreaming will come to terms that the dream and aspirations they were pursuing, were workable. Therefore walk in the footsteps of great minds and taking an action will be as easy as ABC.

7. Act with others in mind

For great people they always believe in teamwork while they share their success story with others. They always leverage to help their dream materialized. Through the support of others, the impossible goals set by them, become reality. As they share their success story bit by bit, they begin to influence people around them. Once they continue to share, their influence extends to people within their community. If they do not relent in their efforts and continue to share unabated, the sky then become their limit and they gradually become a global asset by gaining global recognition. That is why, when the sign of greatness begins in your life, you must try as much as possible to extend a hand of support to help others, who may need your nurturing and mentoring to enable them benefit enormously from the abilities, skills and the interest that God has instil in you.

On the contrary, people who do not have dreams of becoming great, may see this attributes as a time wasting venture. In reality, they may not know that, acting with others in mind, can be a springboard, which may spring them to greatness in the short possible time.

8. Leave your comfort zone

Since great people are tag as movers and shakers of society, they often leave their comfort zone. Outside their comfort zone is where they normally chance on new ideas that lead to the discovery of fresh opportunities that are yet to be utilized.

When they meet new challenges, they end up acquiring new experiences to confront life and finally uncover hidden opportunities. Through these innovations, they end up making the world a better place. That is why, they do what they can, to find themselves in an enabling environment, where their creative abilities, can manifest itself.

9. Surround yourself with the right people

When you surround yourself with people who are prepare to motivate, encourage and constructively, criticize your thought, actions and emotions, little by little, they may strengthen your path to greatness.

These are the people you may need in your life, in order to reach your goals and aspirations. Most often, they bring to the table, positive ideas, constructive criticism and directions that can influence you to have a different mindset. Their actions can influence you to think and act differently, in order to reach your destination.

In view of that, they are prepare to support you, in your quest of making a difference in others life. When they come into your life, they are likely to offer you the needed positive vibes that can push you to attain excellence. As a result, the best in you can easily manifest itself, once you surround yourself with the right people, who may assist you as you toe the line of greatness. If not for anything at all, you will learn from their success and failures to enable you adjust your life accordingly.

10. They think of living a legacy

Great people always want to leave a legacy, for generations to reminisce about when they are gone. This legacy is the biggest impact that they wish to live for future generations. Due to this they are prepared to channel all their resources and forged ahead to ensure that they see the bigger picture in reality. As the saying goes, hard work pays, so by dint of hard work, they often persevere and endure every challenge that come their way until they finally draw closer to the legacy they have planned living. As the major impact or target, they have set to do happen, another burning, sensational and groundbreaking legacy surfaces. That is why greatness does not have an end. When the greatness door of excellence begins in their life, they finally push forward to become, great, greater and the greatest in anything their hands find doing.

11. Stay away from nagging friends

If you allow the words of nagging friends to drain, demotivate and draw you back go, your path to greatness will be smooth. As they quietly leave your life, it will give you the cutting edge to prosper, because new ideas that may surface in their absence will not face any stiff opposition. Although sometimes it may be good to have drainers around, bear in mind that is not everybody who can stand their deliberate discouragement.

In most cases, the words they speak into your vision, are meant to kill your innermost believes by bringing chaos and confusion into the effort you are making. If you are not smart enough, to notice their intentions and allow them to control your actions, their words will finally kill your vision. Once their master plans see the light, it will be difficult for you to make any serious gains in life. These often happen because they know deep within them that, if they do not stop you from pursuing your vision, as time goes on, you may have a competitive advantage over them.

Usually, you will hear them uttering several demotivating phrases, clauses and sentences to restrain you from taken that bold steps that may lead you to greatness. Once you ignore them, your life will be free from major obstacles. You should not be oblivious to the fact that, drainers are not with you, if

you can listen, analyse and evaluate issues based on facts at hand, you will come to terms that drainers are everywhere.

The crux of the matter is that, drainers often surround themselves with people who want to be great. That is why, behind most successful stories, there are often drainers. In fact, if you are not making significant impact or planning to achieve a bigger vision, it will be very rare to see drainers in your life. Most of their words, actions and emotions that they often exhibit when they meet you, become so glaring and intense, when they see potentials in you.

At times, when you clearly, disclose the intentions you have towards achieving greatness to them, all of a sudden, they will turn to discourage you. If you pander to their whims, it will be difficult for you to experience greatness in your life, unless a divine intervention set in.

12. Build a network of people who share your vision

As you begin to experience steady growth, you need trustworthy people who may diligently buy into your vision and support you with encouraging words, phrases and sentences that can inspire you to do more, by putting in your best. What they offer is the exact opposite of what drainers often propose. Their words can spark, ignite and passionately urged you to press on with confidence.

For all you know, your maker may has sent them in your life, to come and augment your little efforts, to see you at the top. If you are not blindfolded but have an open-mindset, locating them and acquiring these benefits will not be tough.

13. Treat your subordinates with dignity

Once you reach your peak, it will be prudent to treat your subordinates well, since they are the ones, who will see to it that, the vision you have nurtured see the light of day.

If you do not treat them with the necessary cordiality, they deserved and they later realize that insecurity, disrespect and depression has taken over the ethics of the company, they may pay back the company in its own coin. These negative feelings can affect the actions and emotions of your subordinates, which may provoke them to adopt a lukewarm attitude towards their daily work. The ramifications of their actions, may affect the company's output in general.

14. When greatness begins, celebrate the little gains

When you experience greatness, be prepare to celebrate the gains, as and when it comes. This will inspire, rejuvenate and give you the needed impetus to press on. If you do, even when challenges crop up, this achievement can boost your confidence level and provide you with the needed impetus to surmount any new challenge that may come your way. Once you celebrate these little gains as and when the need arises, it may rejuvenate you, to maintain your status quo or better still improve upon it without external motivations. Therefore, let the celebration goes on and on, when you finally achieve something great, to

serve as the motive behind your motivation that drives your actions.

How to maintain greatness

Maintaining greatness is an uphill task. It may take consistency, hard work and series of research, before ordinary people, celebrities and institutions, can finally keep their success flame burning. Although, one can examine the success story of others and learn from it, we should not be ignorant to the fact that at times, someone success theory may not work for you, but research shows that in most cases these theories often works.

When greatness begins, there are standards, principles and strategies to adopt, in order to maintain your pace and aspire to great heights as you battle with life each day. Below are the steps needed to maintain the pace to stay at the top.

1. **Don't relent on your achievements, but press on for higher goals**

   At times, when you reach your peak, it is very difficult to maintain the passion you started with, since you may easily be satisfied with, what you have. When your plans and aspirations manifest itself and catapults you to success, do not be complacent. When people become content with their achievements, they seem to forget that, they are living in a competitive world. They forget that day in day out they need a competitive edge to stay competitive, but some great people relent in their efforts and little by little, they lose interest in pursuing their goals. Due to the comfort that they are enjoying, it will be difficult to forge ahead any longer, since they may have all that it takes to relax and enjoy the fruit of their labour. If they continue to relent in their effort towards greatness, in the end it will not augur well for them. Once they realize their pitfalls and begin to press on with all the zeal for a higher goal without stopping, their dream of maintaining greatness will come to fruition.

2. **Don't forget to thank your maker**

You need to give your maker, the needed thanks and appreciation for what he has done in your life, no matter the religion you belong. Do you know that, there are two sides to a coin? So it is life. The life you are living, have the physical side and the spiritual. It takes the two to be a whole being, so when greatness begins, you must try as much as possible to nourish both your spiritual and physical life to enable your life thrives in the midst of challenges. When your little gains usher you to great height you must be prepared to give to Kaiser what he is due and give to God what He really deserves. This will help in strengthening both your spiritual and physical being that will provide you with the holistic assistance you may need as you crave to maintaining greatness.

3. **Invest your gains in other areas**

When greatness begins in your life, try as much as possible to reinvest your gains in areas of your interest, to help utilized opportunities that have not been tapped. This will help you acquire, multiple income. If you acquire extra source of income, it will

give you the ability to influence many people in a more positive way, to help others reach their goals and aspirations. This will give you the extra urge to spread your tentacles to reach many customers who are not within your reach to have the opportunity to patronize your service.

Once your investment reaches untapped areas where competitors are yet to discover, you will soon move beyond your wildest dreams.

4. Research into current ways of doing things

Your continuous stay at the top as a company, after achieving greatness, rest on the premium you placed on research. When you research day in and day out, in search of new ways of doing things, it will then give you a competitive edge, over your competitors, when you chance on new techniques.

Researching into issues, will keep you abreast of current happenings including market trend that can help the company to know what is really trending, when it comes to your focal area, of work. It will also help you to know your target audience, whether they have change their taste or choice, if they have really change, what informed their decision. Aside that, you will get to know what their preference are, and adjust where necessary.

The research should be carry out from time to time, to enable the company plan and strategized ahead of those, who are rubbing shoulders with them. The current ways of doing things, will give the company simplicity, accuracy and speed needed by any company in order to stay at the top.

5. Award creative and innovative minds

Creativity and innovations are the cardinal tools needed by any organization in 21st century to thrive for excellence. Companies and institutions must hit the ground running with creativity and innovations, in order to make inroads into their daily pursuit. These can be made possible, by introducing, an award scheme, that will take charge of creativity and innovation. Once the workers know that recognition awaits them after a hard day's work, the workers will all work with one accord in order to merit these laurels.

6. Invest in technology

Technological advancement in life is crucial when businesses want to outweigh their competitors. Technology is also one of the 21st century tools needed in order to stay current, if you really want to crave for excellence.

Below are some of the advantages that technology brings to businesses, if companies can make conscious effort and implement them their businesses would never be the same.

i. Speed and accuracy

Through technology, organizations can have an automated database, which can give them the progression of the company. With a touch of few buttons, financial report, the demographics of both clients, employees and other relevant information can be generated. For instance, complex data that may take days, months and years to acquire, may

be generated within few minutes and the accuracy that comes with it, speaks for itself.

ii. **Sense of security**

Securing your business is crucial, in the 21st century in which we find ourselves. Businesses can secure their data or relevant information, with the help of software and hardware devices. For instance, Closed Circuit Television Cameras known as CCTV cameras and firewall can help combat data theft and cyber related crimes, which are closely associated with the use of the internet. An issue relating to security is a matter of concern for all and sundry, since security breach can launch a company into trouble. When businesses invest in technology, they will be up to date on new developments that threatening the security aspect of a company and ways to combat them, using current technology.

iii. **Cost effective**

When you compare, the total benefit of IT to your business, you will realized that, after investing in IT over a period, the benefit of IT to the company or institution, will outweigh the total amount used in employing the services of an IT professional. The input of IT expects can help save the business huge sums of money.

iv. **Advertisement**

The role that advertisement plays cannot be underestimated. For instance, a lot of companies and businesses can use information technology, to advertise and sell beyond their boundaries. A typical example is the use of internet and social media, these 21^{s} century tools if well manage, can enhance the prospects of the business. This can be achieved when companies invest in the Internet, by building a website and creating a social media page, like Facebook and LinkedIn.

Aside that, companies can generate more income by creating awareness of their existence through a YouTube channel, Instagram and so on. In addition, Skype can help industries interact with each other at different locations with other businesses and companies through video conference. Educational institutions can also through IT, reach out to numerous distance-learning students across the globe.

Therefore, advertising on the internet can let your cottage industry reach global market without you knowing it. This can help company to expand their horizon, serve others outside their environs and maximise profit.

7. **Invest in labour**

Industries that wants to stay competitive and be outstanding among their peers, must invest in their personnel. From time to time, they can take their staff through refresher courses, to sharpen their skills and revive their minds. This will always keep them tune to the current ways of doing things and be on top of issues when it crops up. Investing in labour will help cut down cost on, obsolete ways of doing things, which are not cost effective. Eliminating awkward ways of doing things can save the company millions

of money, which can be channelled into other areas, the can help grow the business. Check out three benefits to be derived after investing in labour.

i. **It will sharpen the skills and abilities of employees**

   After working for years as a worker, you will gain experience. That does not mean that, you know it all. Refresher course, can equip you, with the current ways of doing things, which may be simpler as compare to the old ways you know, with regard to ways of executing a job. It will expose you to new developments in your area of expertise in order to be effective and efficient in day-to-day activities.

ii. **It makes them feel part and parcel of the company**

   Workers would be extremely happy, if training courses are organized for them from time to time. This will let them know that the company really cares about their welfare and personal development. This goodwill found within the workers, can move the company to a greater height. The benefit that the workers will accrue from the company, may give them a reason to work for long hours without been tired.

When greatness begins in your life, there are things you should avoid. When you finally begin to see greatness in your life, as student, do not relent in your effort else, you will one day loose the passion that drives you to crave for the best in your academic pursuit.

Remember, if greatness was an easy hurdle that is blocking people's way to success, everyone will clear this hurdle and embraced greatness with all the enthusiasm it deserves.

On the contrary, we all know that, it takes conscious effort, to win the battle of greatness, to be a great personality. So, as student, when your greatness begins, do not involve yourself in these five things listed below:

1. **Don't relent in your studies**

   When you achieve greatness in life as student, you must not relent in your effort by thinking that all will be rosy forever. If that happens, you will gradually head towards doom without you knowing it. I will entreat you to take your studies seriously and maintain the techniques and tactics that made you great. Through hard work and perseverance, you will reach great heights.

2. **Don't lower your standard**

   When you long for greatness and it begins in your life as a student, there is one thing that will be prudent not to do. Never lower your standard, if you set a standard and it leads you to greatness never think of lowering it. If you make a mistake and gradually lower a winning standard, you have set for yourself, it will be difficult to continue your winning spree at the top. If care is not taking to maintain the standard that led you to the top, the greatness you admire most will be in shambles.

   Several standards can be set to serve as a regulator, to regulate your life. Without further ado, I

will touch on only two that I deem it essential to every student.

i. **Moral**

If your moral standards come down, the tendency for you to live below the belt will be very high. Since morality means little to you, you are likely to fall prey for any immoral activities that may come your way. This can obstruct your studies and land you in trouble, if not identified early on.

ii. **Academic**

If you lower your standard, in your academic life, your dream of excelling academically and making inroads in the society will be shattered. When it happens like that, most of the things you will do, such as jotting down salient points as the teacher teaches you and following the personal timetable, you have designed to guide and regulate your studies will be in shambles.

Once you lower your standard, these plans enumerated above will suffer failure, since you will not be following it to the latter. If these anomalies are not check, to help you raise your standard, you will end up losing the desire and perseverance to reach great heights.

3. **Don't allow gross insubordination to control you**

When students decide not to abide by the rules and regulations of the school in which they find, themselves, it is known as gross insubordination. The student normally looks down on others with pride and arrogance, while neglecting rules and regulations in any institution in which they find themselves. If it is not detected early on, their attitude will deteriorate later on. This will finally bring the school's name into disrepute. The adverse effects are that, the performance of the student within that particular school will gradually fall.

After experiencing greatness, the onus rest on you to inculcate the words of wisdom, captured in this chapter, in order to stay competitive while securing your stay at the top. If you really want to hold on to greatness each day, then you must constantly equip yourself to enable you stay unique. You must continue to research into issues in order to know the newest trend in business, academia, career and others.

Aside that, the latest software that can assist you to be efficient and effective in service delivery or knowledge acquisition, must be procure. It takes these little things to maintain greatness. It is not a rocket science where adding, subtracting and division can confuse an amateur, to relinquish their long quest of maintaining greatness. When you research into current trends, you will chance on some best practices that you may integrate in your studies and business to help you grow from strength to strength.

Data technology, which seem to be taking the word by storm can aid in several areas of business. Employee skills in data analysis can be sharpened to help them stand the test of time. When data is properly manage, it will go a long way to help the business, to make an informed decision in regards to their client.

They can populate the data to know the range of their target audience, their educational level, to find out, whether

chunk of them are males or female. They can then strategize to make up for the shortfalls if the need arises.

Food For Thought

Once you begin to experience success in your life by reaching the top, you should bear in mind that, there are thousands of individuals, companies and institutions struggling to be there. The onus rest on you to keep the burning desires that sent you there burning unabated. Refusal to do so, you will end up killing your interest, since the little stimuli that drives you to work assiduously to maintain your status quo will vanished.

If you allow positive utterances to fill that empty spaces in your heart, you will only navigate towards good and positive results. In the same vein, allowing positive mindset to preoccupy your mind, you will begin to display positive outcome. When you do, you will radiate self-confidence and be an optimist. From that moment on, you will continue to experience greatness as you stay at the top without qualms.

The believed you have accrued, after reading this book, will equip you holistically as you journey on in life. When the confidences you have acquired radiate your life, let these positive feelings affect the people in your vicinity, your country and the world as a whole. When the efforts you are making begin to have a profound impact on your community, country and the rest of the world, people will hold you in high esteem. Your admirers will make a conscious effort to keep you at the top, since the ripple effect will resonate with them.

Greatness is a lifetime dream of many people, but some don't get there at all. Others at a point in time, bow to the pressures of life and allow the challenges they encounter each day, to crash their lifetime plan. Therefore, once you get there, you must make the necessary effort to maintain the pace that sent you there.

If the plans and strategies that sent you there are maintained and improved upon, the pivotal role you are playing within the company will be noticed. Well, as your greatness begins, I will strongly entreat you to maintain that status quo, with all the passion it deserves, to enable you enjoy the fruit of your labour in your lifetime.

In life, it is great to reach the pinnacle. At the pinnacle is where you may have the resources, the fame and honour that are typically linked with great people. Using it wisely, will help you fulfil the purpose in which your maker brought you to this world. If you do it wholeheartedly without any evilest intentions, you will live a fulfilling life that will transcend your generation.

9 789998 829634